Pub. 1969

# Jack Johnson is a Dandy
# AN AUTOBIOGRAPHY

# Jack Johnson is a Dandy
# AN AUTOBIOGRAPHY

Introductory Essays by
Dick Schaap and The Lampman

CHELSEA HOUSE
PUBLISHERS
New York

# Contents

Salvador Dali's impressions on The Lampman's prized photo of Jack Johnson.

# Preface

Strangely, my admiration and respect for Jack Johnson—not only as a world famous fighter, an outstanding boxer of all time, but as a man—is bound up with my passionate admiration for the great artist, Marcel Duchamp. Perhaps because they were both men of courage, style and imagination, in all ways inspirational, leaders in their respective fields.

Because of the tyranny of time I could have had no meeting with Johnson. Because of the evasions of fate I never met Marcel Duchamp, though I twice came close to it. I would have liked that, as I would have liked to come face to face with Johnson. I would have liked to testify to each one my belief in what he stood for.

Art and the ring may not seem, at first glance, to have much in common, but swiftness, action, adherence without fear to what moves a man, to what his life is, they both have in generous measure. Such qualities endure and influence other men's endeavors in whatever field. And great achievement in art may not be so far removed from ardent and brilliant physical excellence: freedom of spirit and a fresh and powerful demonstration of the artist's vision are at the core of each.

One day in 1966 I was speaking of this with my friend, the painter Larry Rivers, and said, "I love Marcel Duchamp." For answer he gave me Duchamp's telephone number. That I kept, but I never used it. Two years later I sat in the studio of the sculptor John Chamberlain, and he dialed the number intending to arrange a meeting with Duchamp. Chamberlain wanted to photograph me in a special chair belonging to Duchamp, which neither he nor I had ever seen, though we had heard of it from another friend Ultra Violet. But the appointment did not come off, for just then Duchamp was in Europe.

A little after that I was sitting with Salvador Dali in the cocktail lounge of the St. Regis Hotel in New York, and after showing him a prized photograph I had of Johnson, asked him to acknowledge it for me. He took it and disappeared; then, with his usual swiftness returned, ink bottle and pen in hand, and the spontaneous Dalian ceremony took place, witnessed and sealed with a kiss on Johnson's black face by a lovely woman who was present.

I had had the great fighter's Autobiography for some time. I had read it as a child without understanding the complexity of his life, or its essential meaning. But with time I understood both, and guarded the book carefully, certain that the moment would come for it to be presented again, to a public perhaps better able to comprehend that power and tragedy. Chelsea House agreed that this may indeed be the time and was happy to publish *Jack Johnson is a Dandy*. I would like to thank Karen Gullen of Chelsea House for helping to guide the book through the shoals of editing and production.

In Finis Farr's book on Johnson there is the following:

> Off stage Johnson also tried to make a spectacular impression, and at least added the decorative note of fine clothes to the London scene. It is true that the streets were filled with men wearing superb uniforms, and even the eldest of the upper and middle class wore excellent shoes, suits, hats; the world's best. But Johnson's dress during this period was like theatrical costuming. For example, he walked one afternoon down Piccadilly, wearing a biscuit colored silk suit and a pale, golden soft hat, of the style known as the Trilby, after Du Maurier's famous novel. A silk bandana trailed from the pocket of his jacket, and he tapped the pavement with a black, silver headed walking stick, almost prancing in shoes made of doeskin and crocodile. And when not walking, he took the air in a white Benz touring car, its top folded back to display leopard skin upholstery.

At that time Johnson was in exile from America, and exile has many and strange faces, both inside and away from our country. At this time too, Arthur Craven, a giant of a man, who claimed to be the nephew of Oscar Wilde, a Dadaist, and a friend of Duchamp, fought Johnson in Spain and was defeated.

But, speaking of defeat, my final chance to meet Marcel Duchamp was at the Preview of the Modern Museum's Dada Exhibition last Spring. Dali had intrigued Duchamp with the matter of the cross cut in my hair at the back of my head, and Duchamp, who years ago had worn a star in the same way on his, went with him through the tremendous crowds in search of me. Once more fate had a hand, for in spite of the costume I was wearing, a king's robe of red velvet with a cheetah skin fastened to my shoulders, they could not find me. I was, for all intents and purposes, invisible.

Did Jack Johnson, through all the varying passages of his life, feel at times invisible? One can only wonder.


The Lampman
November 18th, 1968.
New York

## He Must Have Been Some Man
### by Dick Schaap

Jack Johnson lived for almost twenty years after completing his Autobiography in 1926, dabbling in dozens of businesses, neither thriving nor starving, his fourth marriage enduring through these years. His pride persisted, but his dignity suffered. Johnson frequently lectured on the lessons of life and fate in Hubert's Museum, the Times Square home of the flea circus; he literally carried a spear in a Metropolitan Opera production of *Aida;* he disputed the ability of Joe Louis, the second black heavyweight champion, and even before Max Schmeling said, "I zee zomething," Johnson spotted the flaw in Louis's defense that would enable the German to knock him out; as late as 1945, Johnson, at the age of sixty-seven, staged a three-round exhibition against Joe Jeannette, the black boxer he had fought three times in 1905, five times in 1906 and once in 1908, in the days when his skills were bright.

Then, on June 10, 1946, in Raleigh, North Carolina, on the way to New York from a lecture tour in Texas, driving too fast as usual, Johnson lost control of his Lincoln Zephyr, skipped across a dividing line, swerved to avoid an oncoming truck and smashed a power pole. Within three hours, the man whom many still consider the greatest fighter of all time was dead.

The death of Jack Johnson revived tales of his battle with Jess Willard—whether Johnson threw the fight, as he insisted in his Autobiography, or whether he simply lost—but the controversy soon faded, and so did memories of the man. In the next fifteen years, as Ezzard Charles became the third black heavyweight champion, Jersey Joe Walcott the fourth and Floyd Patterson the fifth, the significance of Jack Johnson, as the first member of his race to hold the title, diminished. The black man dominated boxing after World War II, and people seemed to forget that the notion of a black champion once terrified segments of white America.

A series of circumstances combined to bring Johnson boldly back to life in the middle 1960's. First, Sonny Liston became the sixth black heavyweight champion of the world. Louis, Charles, Walcott and Patterson had been "acceptable" black men, none openly contemptuous of white society, none flagrantly flouting the rules of that society. But Liston was an ex-con, a drinker, a womanizer, so outrageously "unacceptable" in his background that, the night he won the title, columnist Murray Kempton wryly remarked, "For the first time, an inferior Negro has been granted equal rights." In the pursuit of irony, Kempton had, for the moment, forgotten Jack Johnson, but not everyone had. "If you think Sonny's bad," wrote one sportswriter, "you should have seen Jack Johnson."

If Liston sounded vague echoes of Johnson, the fighter who succeeded Liston as champion, Cassius Clay, suggested far stronger parallels. Clay, like Johnson, had a flair, a streak of eloquence, a touch of class, and, like Johnson, Clay deeply antagonized the Establishment. Just as Johnson stirred racial hatred by parading his affinity for white women, Clay aroused racial hatred first by becoming a member of the militant Black Muslim movement, and second, after changing his name to Muhammad Ali, by announcing that he would refuse induction in the armed forces, that he would not join in the war against North Vietnam and the Viet Cong. For refusing induction—on the grounds that he was a practicing Muslim minister—Ali was indicted, convicted and stripped of his heavyweight championship. He was also stripped of his passport; the government did not want him to slip away the way Johnson had. Although Ali cannot fight in the United States today, he remains, in fact if not in title, the undefeated heavyweight champion of the world. His two successors—Jimmy Ellis and Joe Frazier, each recognized by a different boxing authority —are no more legitimate heirs than Marvin Hart was to Jim Jeffries.

The third circumstance, the decisive one, that raised Jack

Johnson from the dead was the arrival on Broadway of a play called "The Great White Hope," Howard Sackler's drama built around a persecuted black heavyweight champion named Jack Jefferson, a fighter transparently modeled upon Jack Johnson. With James Earl Jones brilliantly portraying Jack Jefferson, "The Great White Hope" was the first solid success of the 1968–69 theater season.

"The Great White Hope" uses as its framework Jack Johnson's life from the day he won the championship, by defeating Tommy Burns in Sydney, Australia, to the day he lost the championship seven years later to Willard in Havana. For the sake of drama, facts have been shifted and distorted. Jefferson's mother, for instance, dies during the period he holds the championship; Johnson's mother died after he surrendered the title. Jefferson is in love with one white woman, and she commits suicide shortly before he loses the championship; Johnson had two white wives while he was champion, and the first committed suicide before he fled the country, almost three years before he fought Willard. Jefferson is almost wholly likeable, a fun-loving, generous, considerate man driven to cruelty only by a society that hates and hounds him, and the white woman in his life is practically a saint; Johnson was not quite so perfect, and the dozens of white women in his life ranged from prostitutes to "nice" girls to celebrities (I am not implying any value judgment as to which were the finer women).

Thousands of Americans who knew nothing of Jack Johnson before 1968, now know him only through "The Great White Hope," and their view, naturally, is distorted. The thrust of the play is accurate—Jack Johnson was the object of blatant bigotry that raised the cry for a White Hope to defeat him—but the particulars, neither in fact nor emphasis, are not. It is, of course, drama, not history, and the playwright has every right to employ only a skeletal truth, especially because he is using the Jack Johnson story to point up contemporary truths.

13

James Earl Jones, in playing Jefferson, concedes that he bases the role only partly on Johnson, partly on Muhammad Ali. And Ali, for all his similarities to Johnson—his quick wit, his grace in the ring, his boxing genius—is a totally different man. Consider just one subject—Jack Johnson's favorite, perhaps—the subject of women.

I remember visiting the young Cassius Clay in Louisville, his hometown, in 1960, shortly after he won the Olympic light-heavyweight title, shortly after he turned professional. He was still in his teens, and he had a wonderful freshness, an engaging directness, and we spent many hours discussing his future, how he would own dozens of Cassius Clay Motels and dozens of pretty cars and everyone would know him and admire him.

And one day we were driving along one of the main streets of Louisville, and I stopped for a traffic light. There was a very attractive white girl standing on the corner, and I turned to Cassius, and I said, "Hey, that's pretty nice." He grabbed my arm, and he looked at me, and he said, "Man, you can get electrocuted for that! A Jew looking at a white girl in Kentucky!"

He was so naturally funny, so relaxed, and then he got into the Muslim movement, and he grew more intense, sometimes taut. He came to believe the Muslim theories of separatism, of white with white and black with black and as little mixing as possible. "The intelligent white man wants white women," he said, "and the intelligent black man wants black women, and that's the way it should be." When "The Great White Hope" became a Broadway hit, someone thought it would be a smart idea to have Muhammad Ali play Jack Jefferson in a touring company, but Ali rejected the proposal. "Johnson mixed with white women," Ali said, with obvious disapproval.

Ali is not a perfect reflection of Jack Johnson, Jefferson is not a perfect reflection and Sonny Liston, of course, lacking in eloquence and in personal style, is not a perfect reflection. Yet all three served the same purpose; all three revived interest in Jack

Johnson, awakened curiosity about exactly who and what he was.

This autobiography amply satisfies at least part of that interest. Johnson tells his story in reasonable detail—he does tend to be repetitious and disorganized—and it is conceivable that he tells his story himself, without the aid of a ghost writer. If someone else did indeed write Johnson's autobiography for him, the ghost's identity has never been revealed. The style seems close to Johnson's; he did speak in a sort of fashionably stilted English, just as the autobiography is written in fashionably stilted English. It is likely that if Johnson did not employ a ghost, he did have the services of an editor, someone who polished his syntax; in speech, if the reports of the time can be trusted at all, and in writing, judging from a few scraps of Johnson's handwritten prose that survive, he was sometimes sloppy with his tenses and his phrases.

Unquestionably, like almost every autobiographical author from Caesar through Hedy LaMarr, Johnson was not meticulous with his facts; for one glaring instance, he remarks late in the book that he held the heavyweight championship for more than seven years and longer than anyone else; the truth is that he held the title for less than seven years and Jack Dempsey held it for more than seven.

As far as Johnson's estimates of his own ability go, he is probably quite close to the truth. Nat Fleischer, the editor of *The Ring,* boxing's most authoritative publication, who has viewed almost every major fight for more than half a century, rates Jack Johnson the greatest heavyweight champion of all. Johnson's special genius was defense; he could pick off an opponent's punch, slap it away with an open hand, then counter immediately with an inside punch. He was a ring scientist in a day of ring laborers.

When Johnson tells of deliberately allowing himself to be knocked down by Stanley Ketchel, he is probably speaking the truth. Most boxing historians feel that Johnson permitted the knockdown, for the sake of a profitable movie sale, before he knocked out the middleweight champion; a few Ketchel admirers, however, insist that the little man actually floored Johnson.

Johnson's argument that he deliberately lost the fight to Willard is less persuasive. He was a shrewd man, wary of almost everyone around him, and it is unlikely that he would have agreed to toss away the heavyweight title without some firm commitment that the defeat would enable him to return to the United States. No scrap of proof has ever been uncovered; the men who supposedly engineered the coup—Jack Curley and Harry Frazee—always denied the allegation. The prevailing opinion is that Johnson took Willard too lightly, neglected to train and went into the ring woefully out of shape. Johnson's later claim that he threw the fight was partly to save his ego and partly to fill his purse. He sold his confession to Nat Fleischer in 1916 for $250. Fleischer did not publish the confession—until 1968—because he didn't believe it. Fleischer, incidentally, saw the fight.

(In "The Great White Hope," the question of whether or not the fight in Havana was fixed is deliberately skirted. Sackler is ambiguous, leaving the audience to choose its own answer.)

Aside from errors of fact and errors of pride, Johnson's Autobiography falls short in one other department. It does not adequately convey Johnson's fine sense of humor. He had a gift for repartee, and while he did not slip into rhymed couplets in the fashion of Muhammad Ali (a fashion adopted by Jack Jefferson in "The Great White Hope"), he could fight and talk at the same time. When Johnson fought Jim Jeffries in 1910, Gentleman Jim Corbett, the heavyweight champion of the 1890's, worked in Jeffries' corner, cheering on the White Hope, trying to needle Johnson.

In the second round, Corbett yelled to Jeffries, with mock amazement, "He wants to fight a little, Jim."

"You bet I do," said Johnson, hitting Jeffries with an uppercut.

Later, Corbett, urging on Jeffries, shouted, "It only takes one or two, Jeff." Johnson promptly hit Jeffries with two sharp punches, paused, then added one more. "See that?" said Johnson to Corbett.

In desperation, as Jeffries' defeat became inevitable and Johnson relaxed and toyed with his opponent, Corbett taunted the playful champion, "Why don't you do something?"

"Too clever, too clever," replied Johnson. "Like you."

It wasn't great humor, but, considering the setting and the more important work at hand, Johnson exhibited an impressive wit.

These samples of Johnson's humor come from the reportage of Jack London, the man who, as much as any other, sparked the search for a White Hope. It was London who, in covering the Burns-Johnson fight, concluded his story, "Jeffries must emerge from his alfalfa farm and remove the golden smile from Johnson's face. Jeff, it's up to you!"

Yet no one in his time, not even London the novelist, was able to capture in print the essence of Jack Johnson. Sports reporters at the turn of the century rarely looked for motivation and character, and no definitive story persists that says this is the kind of man Jack Johnson was. People who knew him in his later years, when he drifted around New York in his jaunty black beret, offered conflicting opinions. Some found him articulate and charming, but many hated him, called him an ingrate, a degenerate, and worse. But all of the harsh words could have been formed by prejudice.

Jack Johnson was a swinger before the term was known. He lived high, surrounded by his retinue, enjoying and apparently satisfying women by the dozens, driving fast cars, drinking good liquor, dressing royally, playing the champion to the core. Imagine the sort of man it took to live *his* life 60 years ago. Even today, in many parts of the country, the mere sight of a racially mixed couple shocks the citizenry. Johnson did it 60 years ago, violating all the codes of the time, leading the sort of life he wanted to lead, defying everyone. It must have taken tremendous courage; people

17

literally wanted to kill him. It must have taken huge native intelligence; he was an unschooled black man out of Texas. He must have been a scoundrel at times, a con man, a hustler; he must have mistreated many people. But think of the forces that shaped him, of the time in which he lived, and accept one conclusion: He must have been some man.

# Jack Johnson is a Dandy
## AN AUTOBIOGRAPHY

# CHAPTER I

## I Take My Pen In Hand

MY name is familiar to a great many people chiefly because I have held the heavyweight boxing championship of the world, and because for more than a quarter of a century I have figured prominently in the making of world ring history. On more than one occasion I have been the central character in sensational episodes which stirred the interest and curiosity of the public. But I am not writing this history of my life—full of experiences and adventures as it is—because of these facts.

On the contrary, in looking back over the years of my tumultuous career, I am astounded when I realize that there are few men in any period of the world's history, who have led a more varied or intense existence than I.* My life, almost from its very start, has been filled with tragedy and romance, failure and success, poverty and wealth, misery and happiness. All these conflicting conditions that have crowded in upon me and plunged me into struggles with warring forces have made me somewhat of a unique character in the world of today, and the story of the life I have led may therefore not only contain some interest if told for its own sake, but may also shed some light on the life of our times.

Quick changes have come into my life on numerous occasions. I have been tossed from one extreme to the other within a few hours. Sometimes I found myself in the midst of disaster and often I arose to unexpected

*John Arthur Johnson was born on March 31, 1878 and died on June 10, 1946.

heights of affluence, power and prominence. Many, many times fortune has virtually dropped into my hands and as many times it has slipped magically from my grasp.

I have attained the peaks of victory in gruelling fights with men as eager, as ambitious, as alert and as strong as I. With these victories generally came great sums of money, sometimes almost more than I ever dreamed of possessing. I was surrounded by countless admiring friends all intent on acclaiming me the greatest in my line; all eager to shout my praises; all striving for my esteem and for my bounty. By a sudden flip of fortune I have seen these friends melt away. But there have been many who have proved staunch throughout the years; who have shared with me in my successes and victories and who have suffered with me in the moments of failure, disappointment and bitterness.

I have known the tremendous exaltation of victory in the ring, in love, in business and in controversies of all kinds, and I have been cast down into the despair that sometimes comes with failure. I have traveled in nearly every country of the world and wherever I have gone I have had adventures that men of my race and nation have never had. I have mingled with notable people of every land. I have been with kings and queens; monarchs and rulers of nations have been my associates. In all the great gathering places of the world where the elite of every nation have met and are meeting, I have enjoyed the distinction of being a celebrity pointed out over all others.

In my life there have been many women, and with women there has come great happiness and also grief and tragedy. Women have come into my life and gone out of it leaving memories, many of which I treasure and many of which I would forget if I could. However, these women whom I have known and loved have been salient factors in my life. They have been the inspiration that urged me to strive for the uppermost places; they have been the cause of situations which turned the eyes of the world upon me, some merely gleaming with morbidness, others flashing condemnation and hate.

I have had my innings with the law. I know the bitterness of being accused and harassed by prosecutors. I know the horror of being hunted and haunted. I have dashed across continents and oceans as a fugitive, and I have matched my wits with the police and secret agents seeking to deprive me of one of the greatest blessings man can have—liberty. And after I had eluded them, after I had spent months in fighting for my cherished freedom and enjoying it at a dearly purchased price, I voluntarily relinquished it and surrendered myself, knowing that I should have to enter prison.

In my fight for my freedom I felt that whatever my conduct had been which led to accusations against me and conviction, it had been no worse than that of thousands of others. I felt that I had committed no heinous crime and that because of my color, perhaps, and because of prejudices and jealousies I was being persecuted and prosecuted. However, after months abroad, always alert lest I should be led into some trap that would mean loss of my freedom, I decided that I would return to my native country, submit to the demands of the law, and clear my "debt to society."

It was this desire to return to my own people and to again look on scenes that I loved and cherished that made my fight with Willard in Cuba, as far as I was concerned,

23

merely an incident, a step in the direction of the goal toward which my heart led me—my home. In order to return to this home and ultimately resume my activities among those who meant most to me I was willing to make any sacrifice. This desire to wipe out prejudices against me and to still criticism of my conduct included my willingness to permit Willard to acquire the heavyweight championship of the world and my consent to go to prison.*

Having disclaimed my intention to write this record of my life because of my attainments in the prize ring or because of the prominence I have achieved in sensational news stories, I wish to go a little further and deny also that I am engaging in this sketch of my life for the purpose of defending myself against charges that were brought against me. I am not attempting this enterprise to explain and excuse my faults and mistakes, nor to win sympathy and smooth over the rough places in my life. On the contrary, I feel that the story of my life is one that will prove interesting and entertaining to my readers as the story of a man, and that it will not be without good results. I am not pointing out any morals, yet when one suffers the inevitable consequences that ensue when the wrong course is chosen or mistakes are made and frankly admits and describes these mistakes and their results, surely it will prove of some benefit if it aids others to avoid similar mistakes and the attending unhappiness and disappointments.

I have no quarrel with fate, nor do I cling to the absurd belief that fate has set any special mark upon me. Yet fate must have intended me for adventures and experiences that do not fall to the lot of the average man. These adventures began early in my life and have

---

* Here Johnson is referring to his 1915 bout with Jess Willard, who knocked him out in the twenty-sixth round.

crowded upon me fast and furiously. I cannot say that I deliberately planned or sought them. Throughout the half century of my life, events have whirled about me in an amazing manner and either engulfed me or lifted me with scarcely any effort or thought on my part.

Of course I had the dreams and desires that are common to youth, but never in the wildest moments of my boyhood imagination did I vision myself the champion fighter of the world, and the first man of my race ever to attain that distinction.* Never did I imagine myself in the picturesque costume of a Spanish matador, a victor in the bullfighting arena surrounded by cheering thousands in the gala attire of the festival in historic Barcelona. How incongruous to think that I, a little Galveston colored boy should ever become an acquaintance of kings and rulers of the old world, or that I should number among my friends some of the most notable persons of America and the world in general! What a vast stretch of the imagination to picture myself a fugitive from my own country, yet sought and acclaimed by thousands in nearly every nation of the world! What an unusual circumstance that while I feared to return to my own country and was a voluntary exile, one of the most notorious revolutionary leaders of Mexico—Villa—was making frantic efforts to finance my return to the Western hemisphere and was attempting to stage in Mexico the championship fight between myself and Willard. How utterly fantastic would have been the thought that I should some day be plunged into romances and love with white women in defiance of a treasured and guarded custom. How far removed from my thought was the possibility that tragedy would creep into my life—the tragedy of a prison term in one instance

* Johnson's heritage was pure Coromantee African stock. His father made his living as a school janitor, but often helped the clergy preach to the Galveston community.

and the death by suicide of one whom I greatly loved in the other.

These are but a few of the unusual events that have come into my life. There are countless others, because I have lived rapidly, intensely, eagerly. I do not recall and write of these things in a boastful spirit, because some of them bring sad memories and arouse regrets; but they have happened and they must be told if one proposes an accurate and candid biography. Of many things I would rather not write for they stir latent sorrows; others, of course, give me cause for pride. There are pleasant topics, too, of which I wish to write, because, happily, my life has not been altogether filled with seriousness and tragedy.

# CHAPTER II

## A STOWAWAY

AS I reflect on the very first adventure of my life, it strikes me as full of humor now. At the time of its occurrence, however, it was painfully serious. One of my earliest ambitions was rather a strange one, and, like many others of my younger years, bore no relation to the course that eventually marked my life. That ambition was to see Steve Brodie, the man who made himself famous by leaping from Brooklyn bridge. Why this fancy seized me I do not know. I was twelve years old at the time and for a boy of that age living in Galveston, Texas, it was no easy matter to arrange a meeting with the daring New York man. From the Texas town to New York was a long way, especially for a youngster without funds and, as I recall it, neither my father nor other relatives were sufficiently interested in my whim to finance a trip to New York. This did not discourage me. I had determined to see Brodie and made several ineffectual attempts to depart from Galveston.

I spent more than a week trying to find a train out of the railroad yards. There were strings of box cars at my disposal and many times, seeing a train of cars moving in the direction which I believed would take me to New York, I hid myself in one of them and settled down for my long journey. When the cars were being shunted about the yards I thrilled with the thought that I was speeding toward the home of Brodie. I rode what seemed many hours in this way and when I imagined that Galveston was far behind me and ventured to peep from my hiding place, I usually found that I merely had been riding about the yards, and when I supposed that probably I was nearing some northern city I was only at some familiar street crossing.

Uncounted times I was driven from the cars by railroad men and some of them were not very gentle in the manner in which they urged my departure from side-door Pullmans. Many of them used their feet in speeding me on my way and I nursed numerous bruises and sore spots. These failures to find my way out of the railroad yards and the painful contact with the heavy shoes of switch crew members did not lessen my desire to make the acquaintance of Brodie. I continued to haunt the railroad yards and to study other methods of reaching New York. Finally I succeeded in stealing aboard a steamship which I believed was bound for New York. Instead its destination was southward. At Key West, however, my journey was rudely interrupted when I was put off the boat. I was penniless, friendless and hungry. It was necessary for me to earn some money so I became a sponge fisherman and incidentally the prey of sharks which infested the waters in which we carried on our search for sponges.

Almost daily our small boats were attacked by the sharks, which was a terrifying experience for me, and one evening when alone in a sailboat, a monster shark 23 feet long attacked me. All I had with which to defend myself was sponge nets and with these I put up a frantic battle, the outcome of which seemed overwhelmingly in the shark's favor, and as the combat went on I became convinced that Steve Brodie was going to be

denied the pleasure of a visit from me. By some miracle
I managed to escape the jaws of the monster until companions came to my rescue and killed my enemy, but
not until after my boat had been almost capsized several
times.

Safe from the shark, I resumed my plans to visit
Brodie and after several weeks as a sponge fisherman,
I found an opportunity to stow myself away on a boat
going to New York. My presence aboard was soon discovered and I was delegated to assist one of the cooks,
my occupation being that of potato peeler. I whittled
many miles of potato peelings probably in a manner not
sufficiently artistic to please the cook, for he treated me
cruelly and lost no opportunity to inflict severe bodily
punishment upon me in addition to the arduous work of
peeling potatoes. One day he beat me unmercifully and
I ran from the hold of the vessel stinging with his blows
and so frightened that I threatened to leap overboard.
In this foolish attempt I was stopped by passengers on
the boat, who, learning of the cruelties to which I had
been subjected, made up a purse for me which enabled
me to pay my fare to New York. Other kindnesses
were showered upon me by the passengers and finally I
reached New York in a fairly prosperous and sound condition. But to the desire to see Brodie had been added
another determination—and that was to find the cook
who had abused me and wreak vengeance upon him. I
promised myself that I would seek him out when my
physical growth warranted it and give him a sound
thrashing, and for twenty years I went about with that
plan in mind, always looking for the cook. Eventually
my anger faded and as more important business engaged
my attention the smarting of the injuries he had inflicted

on me was forgotten. But I have never quite given up the hope of some day meeting my taskmaster of the ship's hold.

Once I was in New York, however, I lost no time in hunting up Steve Brodie. I began by asking the first person who would listen to me after I had landed. To this stranger I addressed my eager inquiry.

"Where is Steve Brodie?" I asked excitedly. He did not know, so I went about firing the question at all who would pause long enough to hear me. I did not so much as provide myself with food or shelter, so determined was I to pursue the quest for Brodie. And it was successful—more successful that I had ever anticipated, for I found at least twenty-five Steve Brodies.

Those to whom I addressed my inquiries, many of them at least, were so interested that they often replied, "That's him right over there," pointing out some man loitering on the corner, or perhaps dashing along the street in a carriage. I took their replies seriously, and on every occasion made daring attempts to make the acquaintance of the man who had been pointed out to me as my hero and idol. More than once I endangered my life by darting across streets unmindful of the threatening traffic, only to find my man had disappeared, or, if I found him, to be met with an angry scowl and a sharp rebuff.

"No, I am not Steve Brodie. Get along with you," I was threatened. On two or three occasions, those I addressed admitted they were Steve Brodie, which lent me a temporary thrill, and a momentary feeling of satisfaction that my life's ambition had been realized. But on each occasion, I learned, to my bitter disappointment, that I had been the victim of practical jokers.

Steve Brodies were beginning to fill my life. I met them at every turn. They went by me in long processions. I dreamed of them when I slept, and day after day I met new Steve Brodies. The disappointments, though, only served to sharpen my determination. I went about hungry and footsore searching for Steve Brodie. So important to me was this self-created mission, that I had made no effort to obtain employment. That I was out of funds did not matter. I ate and slept where and when I could and continued the search. It had one outstanding result. It led to my acquaintance with the be-derbied and box-coated Chuck O'Connor, one of New York's most picturesque characters, dubbed the "mayor of the Bowery," the ruler of the toughs and down-and-outs, the acquaintance and friend of many notable people, and a political power of considerable magnitude during his reign.

O'Connor of the Bowery was first greatly amused at my search for Brodie. He heard the story of my travels with obvious amusement, but he was sincerely interested in me and became one of my best friends. He took me in hand, saw that I was clothed, fed and sheltered, and then sponsored an introduction to the real Steve Brodie, who too became a very good friend. With these new-found friends, I found a new entrance into life, and spent many happy, if not prosperous, days in New York, during which time I met many historic Bowery personages, became more or less absorbed by Bowery life, and enjoyed a small measure of distinction as "the boy who ran away from Galveston to see Steve Brodie."

From New York I went to Boston and worked in the stables of society folk in the Back Bay district. It was here that I experienced a mild tragedy and my career as a worldly young man was temporarily interrupted when a horse which I was exercising, fell with me. My right leg was broken, and I went to a hospital, where I remained for many weeks. When I had sufficiently recovered, friends provided me with funds and I returned to Galveston.

I was now a little past my thirteenth year, but despite my youth, I went to work on the docks, my associates being some of the toughest and hardest-boiled men imaginable. To them, fighting was one of the important functions of existence. They fought upon every occasion and on any pretext. They shot craps and indulged in other forms of gambling with almost as much ardor as they fought. It was up to me to hold my own with them, and I entered into their lives and occupations with as much energy as any of them. Although I was one of the youngest in this rough and aggressive group, I had to do my share of the fighting. It was necessary for me to fight youths much older and larger than myself. I suffered many beatings, but evidently was capable of standing much punishment, for I do not recall that I weakened. I won many of these rough and tumble battles, and because of the ill-matched affairs in which I engaged, I attained more or less reputation as a fighter. It was at this time that I took up boxing, not with any intention of engaging in it as a profession, but because it seemed necessary for me to learn something of the science in order to pit myself against the fighting groups with whom I associated.

One of the memorable fights of this early stage of my life, and one which established my confidence in my fighting ability, was urged on me by my sister Lucy. I had been attacked in the streets by a young man much older and larger than myself. I did not have the courage to fight him, and was casting about for an excuse to evade him. My sister came along at this juncture, and noting that the older boy was taking advantage of me, she became angry enough to demand that I fight him. In fact, she pushed me into the fray. There was nothing to do but fight, and I put all I had in it. The little that I had learned in boxing stood me in good stead, and after a mauling and pounding that lasted for several minutes with the results considerably in doubt, I finally whipped my antagonist. I was considerably surprised, and my friends, hearing that I had vanquished this giant of a fellow, began to praise my fighting ability.

A short time afterward, my reputation went up a few notches further, when I whipped the reigning bully of the docks, a hulking big fellow, feared because of his skill and strength as a scrapper. This was a fight made the fiercer and bloodier, because we were enraged at each other, having quarreled over some money in a dice game. Only a quarter was involved, but since he had snatched the coin from me and made off with it, I was stirred to a frenzied attack and we fought a ferocious battle in which I was the victor.

At about this time I again left Galveston and sought employment which I thought would be better suited to me than the work of a dock hand. In this I was backed by my father, a man of a pious turn of mind, who had served faithfully for many years in the Galveston public schools as caretaker of a school building and preacher in a little church. Neither he, nor my mother and other relatives had been particularly enthusiastic over my activities around the docks. My father would have had me take more interest in the church, and sought determinedly to have me extend my schooling. However, despite my roaming instincts and the hectic experiences I had undergone on the docks, I had not altogether neglected my education, and succeeded in completing the Grammar grades.

In going to Dallas, I had no special plan in mind. I had not decided upon a vocation, and nothing was further from my mind than the thought of becoming a professional boxer, though I had reason to believe that I possessed considerable skill in that direction. In Dallas I found a job in a carriage painting shop, where I wielded the paint brush with more or less success. But here fate stepped in and gave me a push which sent me toward the boxing ring, though I was not aware of it at the time. The man for whom I went to work was Walter Lewis, an amateur boxer of local prominence. He soon learned of my proclivities with the gloves, and enthusiastically set about improving my knowledge of boxing. I was only fifteen years old, but he engaged me in some fast encounters, and I began to have a glimmering of the possibilities of the ring as a career. For six months I manipulated paint brushes and swung the boxing gloves with the fast Walter Lewis and several boxers of varying skill as antagonists, with all of whom I made such excellent showings that I was beginning to make serious plans concerning my future career.

I returned to Galveston, where I was beginning to be known as a boxer, and although I was not yet sixteen years old, my first regular ring battle was arranged. The fight was with John Lee, a boxer who had gained some popularity and who was considered skillful. The encounter took place in a ring built in the open field, and there was a large crowd of fans in attendance. The fight lasted sixteen rounds, and I won. After this, I was matched in several events—in fact was meeting all who were picked by both friends and enemies. But none of these affairs advanced my boxing prestige as much as a fight with another bully and tough of Galveston known as Dave Pierson. This fight, too, grew out of a dice game which was raided one Sunday morning by the police. I was one of the participants in the game, and because I wore my father's overcoat, for which I had been sent to the tailor shop a short time before, I was unable to escape the officers. In a chase that followed, I was overtaken, and in the grasp of two policemen, was being conducted to jail. As we passed along the street, Pierson came into view.

"Here's another crap shooter," exclaimed one of the officers. "Grab him."

Pierson was taken to jail, and in his wrath at being arrested, told the police and others that I was a stool pigeon.

To this accusation, I replied that Pierson was a liar, a dangerous remark unless I was prepared to back it up. Pierson soon heard of it, and among the friends of both of us rumors flew thick and fast. Pierson threatened to "get me," and some of my friends, fearing for my safety, would have had me leave town, inasmuch as Pierson was rated one of the most dangerous men of the town and the most formidable fighter.

The upshot of it was that I was brought face to face with the tough. He asked me if I had said that he was a liar. I told him I had. In a moment the battle was on, and it was a battle without gloves. It was one of the hardest of my life. I was but sixteen years old and Pierson was a grown and toughened man. I fought grimly and as viciously as I have ever fought in my life. I gave him a tremendous beating. News of this fight and the downfall of the bully sped all over the city. A familiar inquiry for several days was,

"Did you hear what 'Lil Arthur' did?"

That was the origin of the nickname which has become so well known in the sporting world. As I came into prominence, and eminent sport writers and cartoonists made me the subject of their articles and pictures, they made frequent use of that name. To "Tad", the famous writer and cartoonist, who became a good friend of mine, I owe much for the inspiration, counsel and public backing which he gave me, and it was he who made the appellation "Lil Arthur" known the world over.*

More and more I was coming to think of the boxing ring as a profession, but had made no definite plans in this direction. My decision to make an attempt to acquire ring honors came shortly after my fight with Pierson, and was hastened when I stayed four rounds with Bob Thompson,† in those days a fighter of considerable prominence. He had whipped some of the hardest men in the ring. He came to Galveston, meeting all comers and paying twenty-five dollars to any who would go four rounds with him.

I took up the challenge, entered the ring with Thompson, and got the twenty-five dollars. I barely stayed the four rounds. At their conclusion I was greatly pleased. It was the hardest earned money of my life, and it was two weeks before I could venture forth to spend it, so great was the beating which Thompson gave me.

* "Tad," Thomas Aloysius Dorgan, was a leading cartoonist-sportswriter and, at the time, was considered one of the best judges of American boxers. He once told Johnson, "Kid, I think you've got what it takes. You're going to beat them all."

† Other sources indicate this fighter to be Bob Tomlinson, not Bob Thompson.

# CHAPTER III

## BREAKING IN

AFTER my fight with Thompson, opportunities for ring activities were few for me in Galveston. Working on the docks, although I was a shipping clerk, held no inducement for me, and I began to look about for something better. I decided to leave Galveston, but had no particular destination in mind. I adopted a simple course and got on a freight train one night as it pulled out of the Galveston yards. I had cast myself wholly into the lap of fate. Although I did not know where the train was bound for, I was not greatly worried over the matter. I did not know where I was going but I was on my way.

On this trip I experienced all the hardships, uncertainties and dangers of freight-train touring. I was without money and there were many days when my stomach shouted angrily for food. Fellow travelers, in the same plight as I, but more familiar with the customs of tramping, initiated me into the secrets of obtaining, here and there, scraps of food sufficient to keep me alive. But hunger was not the only difficulty with which I had to contend. Hard-boiled train crews did not seem enthusiastic over having me as a passenger, and on countless occasions I was chased from boxcars, gondolas and blinds. Brakemen impressed me with their earnestness by brandishing clubs with which they threatened to break numerous bones in my body. Train crews were not my only enemies. In railroad yards, where I lingered

37

watching for an opportunity to board a train that seemed bound for somewhere, road detectives and watchmen lurked, or if I ventured into the streets of some of the smaller towns where a stranger was quickly discovered, police officers and constables manifested deep concern in me. In fact, they were generally so deeply interested that they often insisted that I remain as a guest of their town. On these occasions, I was introduced to the town Judge, who pried into my personal affairs and asked me embarrassing questions. Usually, after my meeting with the Judge, I was instructed to hasten out of town, which was just exactly what I wished to do, and what I was trying to do when the police interfered. Sometimes I was detained, quarters being assigned me in the town jail.

Eventually, after trying out the facilities of several slow, fast and indifferent freight trains, after I had learned the nooks and crannies of many railroad yards and formed the acquaintance of hordes of train crew members, I reached Springfield, Illinois. This city, although made famous by Abraham Lincoln, meant no more to me than any other. I had no particular reason for stopping in Springfield, further than that I was compelled to do so because of the erratic schedules of the trains upon which I rode. However, while making a temporary stop in Springfield, I learned that an athletic club of this city was staging a boxing show, and that the club was in search of fighters to enter a battle royal. I volunteered for the fray and entered the ring more or less fatigued from my arduous travels and the irregularity of my meals.

There were four men in the fight beside myself. I was hungry; my great ambition as the fight began was to eat;

and I feared that if I did not win the fight, I might not have an opportunity to eat. My appetite was my second and backer and I certainly fought—and I won! I knocked out each of my four opponents, which seemed to convince the spectators that I was a fighter of no mean ability.

It so happened that the boxing show, of which the battle royal was a part, was conducted under the direction of Johnnie Connors, who, it will be remembered, was prominent in the boxing activities of that period, and who has been one of the most loyal friends I have ever had. Johnnie was sufficiently impressed with me to take me under his wing, and shortly after the Springfield affair he brought me to Chicago. It was my first visit to the city which was to be the scene of so many escapades of my life; where I was to experience my greatest joys and sorrows and to have some of my greatest triumphs.

Three days after my arrival in the Windy City, Connors arranged a match for me with a fighter known as Klondike, who had attained much success in the ring, and who at that time was a popular ring performer in Chicago. In this fight I was beaten, although half the rounds were mine. The showing I made was sufficient to hold the interest of fight fans and to win many friends and backers for me. The Klondike match netted me a considerable sum of money, a considerable sum for those days, and probably more than I ever had before in my life. The money, however, was soon exhausted, because I undertook to play the races at Springfield, a new form of thrill and amusement for me. I was not clever in picking winners and the proceeds of my first Chicago fight did me little good.

I was now seventeen. Until this time, my plans for

becoming a professional boxer had been more or less vague. The battle royal at Springfield and my encounter with Klondike served to decide me in my course, and I definitely selected the ring as my goal, and for the first time began training in real earnest, and with men more skillful and clever than I had ever met before. There were several of these in Chicago at that time, and among those, who, as I recall it, took the most sincere interest in me and my ambitions, were Dan Creedon and Tommy Tracy. I made sufficient progress in Chicago to encourage me to undertake a trip to New York, where I hoped to meet some of the more notable boxers of the country.

On my way to New York, I stopped at Pittsburgh where a series of fights was being held at the stockyards. I found that as new as I was in the game, I was not altogether unknown in the steel town, and it was not difficult for me to obtain a match, though the man with whom the match was made, was so large and so formidable looking as a fighter, that I had much doubt concerning my chances with him. He was a white man, and in the ring I had the feeling that he was towering over me and was going to make it exceedingly tough for me. The outcome of the fight surprised me, for I knocked him out in five rounds. We fought for a purse; how much, I do not recall. My only recollection is that I left the scene of the fight with my hat brimming full of dollars, and with this small fortune and my victory over the big fellow raising my courage high, I continued my trip to New York. It was my second visit to the city, the first having been when I landed there in my search for Steve Brodie.

I set earnestly about establishing myself in the boxing

game and sought to associate myself with some of the leading boxers of the city. My first overture was made to Bill Quinn, who was then training for his fight with Joe Walcott.* Quinn felt that he could get along without my services, and I found myself facing a series of disappointments. I took part in a few minor ring bouts, but for several weeks, my existence was more or less precarious. I renewed acquaintances which I had made on my former visit, and many of these attempted to aid me in my endeavors to form contacts with boxers and fight managers. Many, it appeared, doubted my abilities and it was difficult to obtain financial backing. I proposed to meet several boxers, but for one reason or another I failed to make any matches of consequence. After the Quinn-Walcott fight my chances brightened up a bit, and I found a place in the camp of Walcott, who had beaten Quinn. With Walcott I went to Boston where I served with him as a sparring partner for two months. All the while, though, I was casting about for a match which would help me along to the goal which was beginning to take form in my calculations, though I was not yet even secretly aspiring to the great championship. While in Boston, I succeeded in arranging a match for myself with Harry Tuttle, afterward prominently identified with the Detroit baseball team. For this match I went to Bridgeport, Connecticut, to train, but the fight never came off, because of Tuttle's failure to appear, as a result of which I was awarded the forfeit.

Friends now began to urge my return to Galveston, where some new fighters were coming into prominence, and therefore, not finding my ambitions coming to immediate realization in New England, I again returned to my home town. Here, I found several boxers had estab-

---

* Joe Walcott, not the "Jersey Joe Walcott" heavyweight champion of the early 1950's, but the Negro welterweight known as the "Barbados Demon," whose boxing style greatly influenced Johnson. Johnson often imitated Walcott's West Indian accent on his lecture tours later in his life.

lished themselves. There was none among them who gained more than local reputation, as I recall it, but some of them were skillful, and I took part in numerous fights, none of which added particularly to my reputation as a fighter. Nor did I profit greatly financially, but I was learning much about boxing and obtained excellent training which was to stand me in good stead in the future events which called for all the skill and experience I could muster. After a year or so in Galveston, during which time I had defeated all the boxers of consequence, I was invited to visit Hot Springs, Arkansas, where for six months I engaged in several ring events, most of which I won, but like my Galveston fights, they netted me little in the way of prestige or money.

I returned to Galveston in 1896. I had reached my 20th year, and had had so many fights that I had lost all track of the number, though there were none of much interest to the public, except perhaps my fight with Klondike in Chicago. As I was only a little more than seventeen at that time, however, it is probable that Chicago had forgotten all about me. Because of my youth, neither Boston nor New York had taken me seriously, although in Boston I had managed to rouse the contempt of some of the Irish gangs of that city, who were still ardent friends of John L. Sullivan, who four years previously had lost the championship to Jim Corbett. I was an admirer of Corbett, and having expressed my opinion of him within the hearing of the Irish fans, I found it necessary to defend myself occasionally against their attacks, and once at least, because of my friendship for "Gentleman Jim," I suffered a severe beating.

Soon after my return from Hot Springs, I fought Howard Pollar, who was attracting considerable attention in the South, and having beaten him, was matched to fight Jim Scanlan of Pittsburgh, for which fight I did real, earnest training. I got the decision over Scanlan and then Klondike came along in 1901, and I went into the ring with him for the second time, the first having been in Chicago, where he defeated me. Our second meeting was different—the decision went to me. By this time Galveston was taking considerable notice of me and there was much activity in arranging matches. After the go with Klondike, I met Jack Lawlor and defeated him, and soon thereafter I took on Joe Choynski, who was attracting national attention, and who, though he had gained no championships, had fought some hard men. The fight resulted disastrously for both of us. I lost the fight in three rounds, because it was stopped by the police.* Both Choynski and I were arrested and held in prison for three weeks, charged with violation of the Texas anti-boxing law in force at that time. As neither of us was successful in obtaining bonds pending what appeared to be an effort to determine how far the law might go in punishing us, we remained in jail. Finally it was decided to liberate us, and, soon after, a special session of the state legislature passed a new law, making prize-fighting a felony.

After this event, Galveston held no great charm for me and I again set out for new fields. My quest took me to Memphis, where for the second time within the year I met and beat Klondike, the Chicago fighter. It was the third appearance we had made in the ring. In the same year I met and defeated Josh Mills, this fight also taking place at Memphis. After that, the Tennessee city offered me little, though I remained there several months and then concluded to try my luck in the west. Denver was

* Actually, Johnson was knocked out by Choynski in the third round. Yet, during workouts while waiting for their three-week jail sentence to end, Choynski taught Johnson much of the fancy footwork and block punches that became characteristic of the champion.

my first important stopping place and here I came in contact with some notable fighters. I joined a motley crew of scrappers who were training at Ryan's Sand Creek house, among them being Tom Sharkey, one of the ring's greatest fighters, though he never held a championship. A year or so before he had fought a great battle with Jim Jeffries,* a twenty-round contest at Coney Island, which was one of the longest and hardest in which Jeffries had participated. Also, at Ryan's rendezvous, was Young Corbett who, a little later, acquired the featherweight world's championship by whipping the "Terrible Terry McGovern" at Hartford, Connecticut.

Denver at the time was staging some fast fights in the old Coliseum, but there were no boxers in the heavyweight class available for these events, and I had no opportunity to demonstrate my abilities in the mountain town. Things were going slowly for Sharkey also, so he conceived a plan to organize a big boxing show, which was to take to the road giving exhibitions in fistic science, and which also would meet all comers, in any division of fighting weights. Included in the personnel of this organization, besides Sharkey, were men who had attained more than passing prominence in the ring, or who were destined later to attract world-attention. Among them were Young Corbett, Spider Kelley, Abe Attell, New York Jack O'Brien, who was then lightweight champion of the world, Philadelphia Tommy Ryan, George Dixon and myself.

The finances of the organization being low, we selected a nearby scene for our exploits, the place being Cripple Creek, Colorado, then one of the world's greatest mining camps, where miners and prospectors, sportsmen, gamblers and adventurers of all kinds were gathered,

---

* James Jackson Jeffries won the heavyweight championship in the 1899 knockout bout with Bob Fitzsimmons. He held the title for five years. Still undefeated, he went into temporary retirement. It was believed that no man could defeat him, until the Johnson-Jeffries fight, July 4, 1910, when Johnson utterly destroyed him.

and where wild-west scenes were being enacted daily. We were accorded a rather warm welcome in the gold town and our initial exhibitions were well attended and the box office receipts were satisfactory for a few days. We entertained one aspirant for the heavy-weight boxing championship in the person of Mexican Pete who was creating somewhat of a furor in the west because he had beaten Sharkey. He took advantage of our offer to meet all comers and I was next delegated to meet him. We put on one of the best fights the mining camp had ever seen if hard fighting is counted for anything. It lasted twenty rounds and resulted in my knocking out the aspirant.

It was in Cripple Creek that my first real trouble descended upon me. The morning after my fight with Mexican Pete, a dispute arose between my first wife and myself, and she left me, going to Denver.* This disconcerted me more or less, because it was a tragic circumstance, as such incidents always are in the lives of newlyweds. Ours had been a real love affair and we had been devoted to each other. I was reduced to a gloomy state of mind. Adding to my domestic eruption, came the sad realization that Sharkey's organization of boxing geniuses had gone on the rocks. Our show, it appeared, was a topnotcher, but the mining camp population was not sufficient to maintain us as a profitable going concern. Our expenses had been larger than our income. It was necessary for us to leave our comfortable hotel quarters and find other shelter. We rented a shack of a house in which we set up a co-operative home. In this establishment, I, the conqueror of Mexican Pete, and entertaining high hope of recognition as a master boxer, became the cook. Not only was I delegated to prepare the

---

* This was Johnson's first wife, Mary Austin, a Negro girl from Galveston.

food for the lusty, hungry human machines of flesh and brawn, but it also was necessary for me to engineer the finances and obtain money and credit sufficient to stock the pantry.

The purse was slender and the pantry was scant. Empty stomachs demanded to be filled, and I set about the task with considerable difficulties staring me in the face. I managed to open a credit account with a butcher, who for a time was a source of supply. But as our indebtedness mounted, the butcher grew less obliging; he not only grumbled about the laxity with which he was paid, but he took advantage of our emergency and wished on us an inferior quality of market products. These we accepted and consumed heroically for a time, but when the butcher, in the hope that we would discontinue our patronage, supplied us with ancient and rotten chickens, and my star boarders began to entertain doubts as to my fitness as a cook and ability as a food buyer we complained. However, we did not cease to deal with the butcher, for he was the only one with whom our credit was good, and it was good with him principally because he feared to deny a bunch of fighters, rather than because of faith in our financial soundness.

Eventually the boys, one by one, financed themselves and left the camp. I returned to Denver, where I was reunited with my wife, and hope and happiness again returned. We left Denver shortly afterward and went to Los Angeles, where I met Young Corbett, who, having defeated Kid Broad in Denver, in May, 1902, was preparing for his fight with Terry McGovern, which took place in San Francisco in March, 1903. I busied myself around Corbett's camp and gave the fighter such help and advice as my own experience and knowledge afforded.

In the meantime I was doing some heavy training myself and on the lookout for matches with men in my
class. I mixed with the boxing fraternity in most of the
Pacific coast towns, and, on a trip to Bakersfield, met
Frank Corella, who became my manager. My stay on
the coast was marked by some of the first important
fights of my career. It was also significant because on
March 31, 1902, I won the world's light heavy-weight
championship from George Gardner,* in San Francisco, in
a twenty-round battle. Before gaining this title, I had had
a fight at Oakland with Joe Kennedy who had been one
of Jim Jeffries' principal sparring partners. I won by a
knockout in four rounds.

In the same year I also had fought and defeated Jack
Jeffries, brother of Jim, in a five-round go at Los Angeles.
I had had two severe fights with Hank Griffen who held
a decision over Jim Jeffries, when the latter failed to
live up to an agreement to knock him out. Both these
fights were in Los Angeles and both resulted in a draw.
One went twenty rounds and the other fifteen. In sum-
ming up my fights, throughout my career, there were
none, even in the championship bouts, which were harder
than those with Griffen, and I believe that the greatest
punishment I ever received in the ring was at the hands
of Griffen. Other important fights on the coast, besides
those just mentioned, included a twelve-round bout with
Frank Childs at Los Angeles; eight rounds with Fred
Russell at Los Angeles and twenty rounds each with
Denver Ed Martin and Sam McVey. All of these contests I won.

During my stay on the coast, I had many experiences
and adventures outside the boxing ring, of which I shall
have something to say later. Concerning one, I am go-

---

* This man was the light-heavyweight George Gardiner. Johnson reputedly trained
for this fight on a mixture of brandy and champagne at the suggestion of a British
military officer he met in San Francisco. But, the drink gave him dyspepsia and he
was forced to live on orange juice and milk for three days before the match.

ing to digress sufficiently here, because it made a lasting impression on me—an impression that was heightened by events in subsequent years of my life. Frequently I have been asked whether or not I am superstitious. For the most part, I am not, that is, in the general under-standing of the term. This adventure of which I am writing was with a fortune teller in Los Angeles whom I visited in the guise of a working man. I was careful, or thought I was, to conceal from her the real nature of my occupation. But I did not fool her. She at once told me that I was a boxer, and recounted some of my past life with such accuracy that I was astounded. She pro-ceeded to tell me many things concerning my future, some of them so fantastic and so improbable, viewed from the place I then occupied in life, that I departed from her presence feeling that she had drawn a highly imaginative picture of my life. She predicted that I would be the heavy-weight boxing champion; she told me of my forthcoming marriages and of various affairs that I was destined to have with women; she told me, al-most in detail, of the adventures and travels that were to mark my later life; of my conflicts with the law; of the accident which nearly cost my life in Spain, when an automobile turned over with me; of my sickness, which nearly ended in my death; of my return to America and the events of the following years. I did not give serious attention to her predictions at the time, but within a few years things began to happen that set me thinking and caused me to watch my step. In the years since, events and circumstances have come to pass with little deviation from the manner in which she foretold them. I still do not make an admission of being super-stitious, but as the record stands, the Los Angeles fortune teller still looms conspicuously in my memory, and there are few developments in my life that do not in some way echo that incidental visit, many years ago, when I stood on the threshold of a life that was to be one of the most picturesque in American history.

After my fights with Martin and McVey, early in 1903, I left the coast for Boston, and in April won a ten-round fight with Sandy Ferguson in the "Hub." In May, I knocked out Joe Butler in three rounds in Philadelphia, and in July in the same city, fought again with Ferguson, the meeting going six rounds to a no-decision.

In the fall of the same year I returned to California, and in October won my second twenty-round go with McVey. Ferguson also had ventured into the Pacific coast fight territory, and on December 11, I fought him for the third time and won in twenty rounds.

As far as my boxing activities were concerned in 1904, the year was rather a dull one. While I traveled over the United States considerably and appeared in many minor engagements from Philadelphia to Los Angeles, I had only four bouts of much significance. One was with Black Bill, a six-round no-decision event in the Quaker City, in February; in April, I fought Sam McVey for the third time, the contest taking place in San Francisco and going twenty rounds to a knockout in my favor. In June I won a six-round bout with Frank Childs in Chicago, the meeting being the second one between him and me, and in October, I met Denver Ed Martin for the second time in Los Angeles, and disposed of him in the second round.

One of the busiest boxing years of my life was that of 1905. In all, I had thirteen contests of considerable importance, inasmuch as they convinced boxing authorities and boxers that I was a factor that must be reckoned with in boxing history. In March, in San Francisco, I fought Marvin Hart, who later claimed the heavy-weight championship on the retirement of Jeffries.* This fight was not an auspicious event for me, as Hart got the decision, owing, as Tad, the famous sportwriter says, to the fact that in the excitement the referee pointed to the wrong man. However, it was the only contest I lost, the other twelve events being in my favor, excepting five no-decision matches. These, although they are not officially recorded, were won by me.

During this year Philadelphia was the principal scene of my activities, though I did much traveling. In all, ten fights were staged in the Sleepy City, with me as one of the principal contenders. The first was with Jim Jeffords whom I knocked out in four rounds. I won a four-round affair with Black Bill with whom I had previously had a no-decision bout; I knocked out Walter Johnson in three rounds and went six rounds to a no-decision with Joe Jeanette. I knocked out Morris Harris in three rounds, had another no-decision session with Black Bill; a similar six-round venture with Jack Monroe, the Montana miner who had gained distinction by knocking down Jim Jeffries, and also a no-decision bout with Joe Grimm. At Chelsea I fought and won again from Sandy Ferguson; at Baltimore I knocked out Young Peter Jackson in twelve rounds and concluded the year with a second no-decision match with Jeanette.

In 1906 Jeanette and I mixed our fists and skill no less than four times. On January 6, at New York, we had a three-round no-decision contest; on March 15, I won over him in a fifteen-round match at Baltimore; on September 20, we went six rounds to a no-decision at Phila-

---

* Hart won the title by defeating Jack Root in 1905. Jeffries, referee of the match, proclaimed Hart his successor. In 1906, the 5'7" Canadian Tommy Burns defeated Hart, the title was given to Burns. At this time, Johnson challenged Burns many times but was turned down because of his previous loss to Hart.

delphia and on Nov. 26 we fought a ten-round no-decision bout at Portland, Maine. I knocked out Black Bill in seven rounds at Wilkes-Barre, April 19. I won from Sam Langford in fifteen rounds at Chelsea, Massachusetts, on April 26, and a short time afterward, Langford and I put on an exhibition bout for the benefit of the sufferers in the San Francisco earthquake and fire. I had a one-round affair with Charlie Haghey at Gloucester on June 18, and on November 8, met Jim Jeffords again, winning from him in six rounds.

The end of 1906 found me looking confidently ahead to the time when I should gain the world's heavy-weight championship. I was twenty-eight years old and I had been fighting just about half that time, if I include my boyhood encounters in Galveston. While these, of course, were in no wise to be considered as a part of my record as a boxer claiming championship ability, they nevertheless helped to provide me with a background on which I based my own calculations and aspirations. As early as my sixteenth year, I had met men who claimed prize ring honors and as there had been none who had beaten me severely, and as I had won most of my fights, both in and out of the ring, I felt reasonably certain that there was nothing to block me as far as my skill was concerned.

The five-year period ending with the close of 1906, found me with fifty-six registered fights to my credit, to say nothing of countless matches, exhibition and otherwise, in which I had participated and which were not officially recorded. Of these fifty-six fights, I lost only two—those with Choynski and Hart. In this time I had met and defeated some real contenders, and I think there should have been no denial of my right to contest for championship honors. While sporting writers and boxing authorities still continued to question my claim to higher ring honors, it certainly was not because my record as a boxer was in any wise questionable. I had demonstrated my strength, speed and skill, but still faced many obstacles, the principal one of which was the customary prejudice because of my race. Had it not been for these prejudices, which I shall not discuss here, I think I would have been instrumental in making an entirely different history of boxing in the United States and the world, from that which has been recorded. With the beginning of 1907 I had attained a success that I believed entitled me to propose myself as an aspirant for the championship. Tommy Burns held the coveted honor and I began to direct my attention toward him. It was two years before I got to him and proved my abilities by winning the championship.

Those two years were arduous ones. I struggled diligently in backing up my contentions and I fought in many hard ring events. I took on every potential contender between myself and the champion. I virtually had to mow my way to Burns. I made offer after offer. I proposed all sorts of inducements and made every possible concession. Most of the sport authorities of the world, I believe, recognized my claims and my ability. Even King Edward of England was disgusted with Burns' tactics and called him a "Yankee Bluffer," and went so far as to suggest that unless Burns met me on a fairer basis than he at first proposed, the fight between us, which at one time was talked of as a project to be staged in England, should be prevented.

I am leaping considerably ahead of my story, however, if I am to follow a chronological order. There were, as I have intimated, several hard fights intervening. There were two trips abroad, one to Australia in 1907, and another to England in 1908.

Both these trips were memorable ones. Wherever I went, in either country, I was accorded a warm welcome and in many instances jubilant receptions greeted me. These trips, I believe, had much to do in convincing the boxing world that I was a logical contender for the heavy-weight crown. During this period sport writers and cartoonists were filling many columns about me, and I was the target of enough good natured jibes and jests to fill a volume and a large one at that.

In Australia I settled a dispute over the heavy-weight championship of that country by defeating both disputants. They were Peter Felix, a colored fighter, and Bill Lang. I knocked out both of them, Felix at Sydney, New South Wales, February 19, in one round, and Lang at Melbourne, finishing him in nine rounds. I remained in Australia several months, during which time I made many friends, who, with thousands of others, were to welcome me back in December of 1908, when I defeated Burns.

One event in Melbourne, which brought me $15,000 in an unexpected manner, took place when I unknowingly and unintentionally bet hundreds of dollars on a horse race. The dollars and the betting on my part were imaginary, but nevertheless they won real, hard money. I arrived at the race track in a depleted condition financially. The horse on which I was betting belonged to Jim Brennan, who was the promoter of the Johnson-Felix fight, and whose guest I was in Australia. I saw his horse, Istria, and liked it so well that I bet my last five dollars on it. At the conclusion of the race I collected my winnings amounting to one hundred dollars, then strolled around the track until the races were finished, when I returned to my training quarters. On the next morning, a Sunday and my birthday, I took a trip to Tattersals, where all of the large bets of the previous day are paid. Upon my arrival a man approached me with a huge roll of bills. He handed them to me much to my amazement. But as usual in such rare instances I reached out and accepted the money. Other bookmakers followed him and I accepted their rolls of bills in a dazed sort of manner, for I had absolutely no idea what it was all about.

Finally, one of the bookies told me, as he handed me a wad of bills, "I say, Mr. Johnson, but you were lucky to bet on that horse." I then realized that on the previous day as I was greeting friends and acquaintances with a wave of the hand the bookies took this as a signal to place another bet on my horse. I finally had to provide myself with a handbag to carry my money and when I arrived at home and finished the counting of my newly and unexpectedly acquired fortune I found that the greeting of my friends on the previous day had made me $15,000 richer.

Nothing could have been more opportune for I had been in a predicament for several days wondering how I was to finance my trip back to the United States. If the long shot had not won—well it still makes me sweat to think about it. I would probably have been in Australia yet, wondering what had happened to me and making futile explanations to prison keepers.

Soon after this windfall I returned home. In seeking for more matches I was booked to meet that good old fighter Bob Fitzsimmons.* It was a fight that resulted

---

* Fitzsimmons, in his middle forties when he met Johnson, was heavyweight champion of the world from 1897 to 1899 and light-heavyweight champion from 1903 to 1905.

pitifully, the grand old man of the ring going down for the count in the second round. I do not take much credit to myself for this bout, but it seemed necessary at the time in clearing the course that was before me. On August 28, I knocked out Kid Cutler*at Reading, Pennsylvania, in one round. At Bridgeport, on September 12, I won over Sailor Burke, and my fights of 1907 ended November 2, when I knocked out Jim Flynn in eleven rounds at San Francisco.

---

* Kid Cutler was a protégé of John L. Sullivan. Sullivan had a low opinion of Johnson because of his affairs outside the ring, and believed that Cutler could "chase Jack Johnson out of the ring."

# CHAPTER IV

## FIGHTING TO THE TOP

IN the early part of 1908 I devoted myself to negotiations for matches in which I could prove my skill and win sufficient prestige to be in a position to demand a go with Burns for the Championship. But since there were not many available fighters in my class at the time, I engaged in several minor ring events and continued to keep myself in condition for the big opportunity which I knew must come.

After a few months of comparatively little action, I set sail for London, accompanied by Sam Fitzpatrick, who was filling the post of manager for me. While I met a few of the English fighters and filled impromptu music hall engagements,* the principal purpose of the trip to England was to arrange a match with Burns for the championship, which, for a time, promised to take place in England. Although I made every conceivable concession to Burns we were a long time coming to any terms, and ring history, I believe, will reveal that the preliminary negotiations for that fight required more time and involved more discussion than ever characterized any previous similar event. At times it grew bitter and the press was loud in its criticism of Burns for his long side-stepping of me. In June of 1908, while the bickering was on, I met Al McNamara, a British contender. The contest took place at Plymouth and I won in four rounds. In the following month I fought Ben Taylor, also at Plymouth, and knocked him out in the eighth

---

* Johnson danced and played the harmonica and bass fiddle. Although he was not considered a big stage attraction during his early career, after he won the championship, the music halls were filled with audiences wanting to hear stories of his picaresque life.

round. These contests were merely incidental but they helped me in removing any possible contenders that might remain between Burns and myself.

Finally, to my great satisfaction, the meeting with Burns was arranged to take place in Sydney, New South Wales, Dec. 26, and after a short stay in Europe I went to Australia to begin my training for the bout which I had so long sought and which meant so much to me. In Australia I was warmly received, notwithstanding the fact that Burns was the favorite in the betting, which was to be expected because of the racial element involved. On my first visit to that country I had made many friends and these came hurrying to renew acquaintance with me. I found that I had new admirers also, and the utmost kindness was shown to me on every hand. There were, of course, some outbreaks of bitterness and there was much criticism of both Burns and myself. But whatever hostility was shown toward me came from sources of no great importance, principally those of narrow and bigoted opinions.

Another concession I made in this fight was that McIntosh, Burns' manager should act as referee. Burns had insisted on naming the referee, and I was determined that he should not, but rather than cause disagreement or any room for doubt I assented to McIntosh, Burns' manager and promoter of the fight, so sure was I that there would be no dispute over the nature of my fighting and the results. This was the first time in the history of the ring that one of the contestants' managers had also served as the referee.

By the day of the fight my friends and supporters had increased and Burns was less a ruling favorite. The fight was attended by 30,000 people, who came from every country in the world. It is said that the representation of the press was the largest that ever watched a fight up to that time, countless newspapers and sporting publications having sent their writers to the fray. We fought for a purse of $35,000, and of this amount I got only $5,000, those being the unequal financial terms which I had accepted in order to bring the fight about. I was scheduled to go twenty rounds but the fight was stopped by the police in the fourteenth round, so obviously was it in my favor. I was declared the world's champion heavyweight boxer. The fight was one of the easiest of the more important fights of my career. At no time did Burns have a show with me. The champion had fallen. A new champion had arrived and that new champion was Jack Johnson.

I had attained my life's ambition. The little Galveston colored boy had defeated the world's champion boxer and, for the first and only time in history, a black man held one of the greatest honors which exists in the field of sports and athletics—an honor for which white men had contested many times and which they held as a dear and most desirable one. Naturally I felt a high sense of exaltation. I was supremely glad I had attained the championship, but I kept this feeling to myself. I did not gloat over the fact that a white man had fallen. My satisfaction was only in the fact that one man had conquered another, and that I had been the conqueror. To me it was not a racial triumph, but there were those who were to take this view of the situation, and almost immediately a great hue and cry went up because a colored man was holding the championship.

The hunt for a "white hope" began, not only with great earnestness and intenseness, but with ill-concealed bitterness. I regretted this phase of the hunt. Many times there was manifested by those from whom we should expect better things an unsportsmanlike attitude that I regretted then and always shall. That they should wish to find a contender for the crown was natural and I lost no time in announcing my readiness to meet any who might wish to strive for the honors I had attained. There were many possibilities in the field. Burns, my late defeated antagonist, soon after our meeting, set forth to comb Europe and other sections of the world for someone whom he might send against me in an effort to win back what he had lost. Everywhere the search went on.

I watched it with deep interest but not with any alarm. I was sure of myself and would have taken the utmost satisfaction at any time in giving aspirants an opportunity. In the meantime I returned to the United States, having remained in Australia only a few days after the championship battle. I was accorded the utmost consideration wherever I went and much pressure was put forth to induce me to remain longer. Several celebrations were arranged in my honor. In Western Australia a special race meet was put on for me; a whippet race also was one of the entertainments provided for me and party, and I left Australia with the very kindliest of feeling for that country and its people. As I boarded the ship on my return home I was loaded down with gifts.

After crossing the Pacific I spent a few days at Vancouver and San Francisco. Ovations were tendered me everywhere. I made a brief stop in Chicago on my way to New York, and in the former city, which by that time had come to be my home, I received a tremendous welcome. After a short visit with my relatives I hastened to New York, where I signed a thirty-week theatrical engagement with Hammerstein, providing for several tours which took me over a great part of the United States and Canada. My theatrical work, of course, included boxing exhibitions, and for that reason I was constantly in good trim and ready almost any time to enter the ring. Between stage appearances I had some minor ring affairs. One of these was with Victor MacLaghlen* in Vancouver, March 10, 1909, which I won in six rounds. Another was with Philadelphia Jack O'Brien in Philadelphia, May 19. Although O'Brien was being grooomed as one who might take the championship from me, the result of the fight, while no decision was given, clearly showed that O'Brien would have to be eliminated as a contender. Following O'Brien came Tony Ross, with whom I entered the ring in Pittsburgh, June 30. We fought six rounds to a no-decision conclusion, but the outcome was unmistakably in my favor. About this time the giant fighter Al Kauffman, appeared on the horizon, and in him were placed the hopes of those so eager to have a white man again wear the championship belt. After considerable negotiations, articles between Kauffman and myself were signed and the fight took place in San Francisco September 9. It went ten rounds. Officially no decision was rendered, but I had so much the best of it throughout that Kauffman was removed from the list of eligibles without any dispute. One more hope remained—Stanley Ketchel,† who, it was firmly believed by some, would whip me. We fought at Colma, California, October 16, 1909, and I knocked him out in twelve rounds. After this fight I returned to Chicago and bought a home for my mother

---

* Victor McLaglen afterwards won an "Oscar" for his role in "The Informer." He was the only "Oscar" winner who ever had fought for the world heavyweight title.

† Ketchel was the world middleweight champion. Johnson outweighed him by thirty-five pounds.

and her family. I spent the holidays with my relatives and after Christmas returned to New York, where I was booked for more theatrical engagements.

With the downfall of Kauffman and Ketchel, all immediately available contestants for the championship were disposed of. The demand for a white champion was growing louder every day, and many promoters were diligently searching for someone to pit against me. Jim Jeffries, once champion, one of the hugest and hardest fighters America ever produced, had retired. He had voluntarily relinquished the belt to Marvin Hart, who had been whipped by Burns. Therefore it was believed that Jeffries was in reality the champion, and whether or not he did hold that honor, it was declared he was the only logical man to send against me. For a long time he refused to fight me, contending that he was through with the ring, but ultimately friends and the demand of the public prevailed on him and he consented to meet me.

Tex Rickard and Jack Gleason got together and arranged to promote the fight, offering a purse of $101,000. Articles for the encounter were signed between us in Hoboken, February 1, 1910. Immediately upon signing of the articles, Jeffries took advantage of the publicity which the forthcoming fight occasioned and made several profitable theatrical engagements. He was now termed the "undefeated champion," notwithstanding that my fight with Burns gave me the recognized official title. This fight attracted more attention than the Burns encounter. There was a strong belief that Jeffries, having never actually been whipped, would regain the title. There was much bitterness preceding the fight and every effort was brought to bear to strengthen Jeffries with the public as well as to condition him for the bout.

# JACK JOHNSON

For some time I continued my theatrical engagements and on May 15, after another visit with Chicago friends and relatives, I gathered my party and went to San Francisco, where it originally was planned that the fight was to be held. After I arrived on the scene preparatory for my training, the California governor decided that he would not permit the fight. Thus interrupted, Rickard and Gleason sought another location, and after considerable delay selected Reno, Nevada, setting the date for July 4, 1910. When the day of the big fight arrived I was in the best condition of my career. I had trained conscientiously and meant to do my very best. It was likewise announced that Jeffries' condition was perfect.

The ring was built in the outdoors in the center of a natural amphitheater. It probably was the most picturesque fight scene ever staged in the history of boxing. A tremendous crowd was in attendance and there was a suspense that at times was almost unnerving. The fight meant more than any that had ever taken place among heavyweights. My staunch and eager friends were numerous but there was a bitterness against me that probably was more manifest than upon any other occasion. Rumors had come to me that there actually was talk of a chance shot at me if I whipped Jeffries. It was hinted that gunmen had been hidden in the crowd and that if my boxing opponent did not dispose of me a bullet would. I took little stock in this. I could not imagine any sportsman sunken to such depths, yet such rumors served to indicate the hostilities that existed. When the fight began and as it continued I was jeered by my enemies and cheered by my friends. The taunts I received were calculated to disturb my poise. But these efforts failed. A red hot sun poured down upon our heads. The great crowd was burning to a crisp. One can easily imagine what gruelling it was for us battling in the ring. However, despite the sun and the jeering mob and the occasional thought that there might be a gunman somewhere in that vast array of humanity, I do not recall that I was greatly disturbed. "The golden smile" for which I have become famous, I am told, never deserted me, and there was no reason why it should have. Jeffries at no time made the going very difficult for me, and in the fifteenth round I knocked him out. Whatever possible doubt may have existed and did exist as to my claim to the championship was wiped out. I had again demonstrated the material of which I was made and I had conclusively vanquished one of the world's greatest boxers. In the gathering of spectators who saw the encounter was another huge group of newspaper writers and photographers, and round about us telegraph instruments clicked off a description of the fight blow by blow. I recall that occasionally I took time during the exchange of these blows to suggest to telegraph operators what to tell their newspapers.

Notwithstanding the long years I had been boxing and the numerous fights I had been engaged in, the Jeffries fight brought me the only real money I had ever made out of my profession comparing the purses of those days. I got 60 per cent of the purse, or about $60,000. A bonus of $10,000 was given me and the picture rights netted me another $50,000 or about $120,000 in all. After this fight I believed that the bitterness which had actuated some of those interested in boxing had subsided. Some of my greatest enemies were silenced and many who had been almost venomous toward me grew a little more restrained. None could deny that I had fought persistently and conscientiously. I had won all I had attained by sheer hard training, fighting and confidence in myself. Back of that confidence was the faith of my friends and the belief in me of my mother who, when told of both my victories—that in Australia and Reno— expressed no surprise. She said she knew that I would win.

More theatrical contracts and long tours over the United States and Canada followed the Reno fight. And with these engagements completed, I determined to take a rest, which took the form of a trip to Europe. With me on this trip went Bob Armstrong, Kid Cutler, my wife, formerly Etta Duryea,* my nephew Gus Rhodes, and my chauffeur. While I intended that this trip should be for nothing but rest and pleasure I found that my popularity in Paris and London had increased to such an extent that there were insistent demands for my public appearances, and much against my will I appeared in several music halls and theaters in both capitals in boxing demonstrations.

While I was in London on this occasion, the coronation of King George V was in progress. London was jammed with the throngs that had come from all over the United Kingdom and nearly every country in the world. Despite the fact that the King and his coronation were the center of attention, when my car traveled along London streets and it was announced that I was in sight, the attention of the crowds was turned upon me, and as long as I was in view the coronation ceremonies were forgotten while crowds milled and struggled for a glance at me.

My visits in France and the United Kingdom were

* Johnson met Etta Duryea at the Coney Island Race Track and married her in 1909. She was his second wife, and his first white wife.

Jack Johnson and his mother "Tiny" Johnson, who urged him to leave the country rather than face up to a jail sentence for violation of the Mann Act.

Johnson and Tommy Burns fight for the heavyweight championship in Sydney, Australia, 1908. Johnson won the title by decision in the fourteenth round.

UNITED PRESS INTERNATIONAL

Jack Johnson, the first black heavyweight champion of the world, held the title from 1908 to 1915.

Jack Johnson and his second wife, Etta Duryea Johnson were married in 1909. They toured Europe and the U.S. together.

On Johnson and Etta's return to the U.S., they opened the Cafe Champion in Chicago. It was here that Etta committed suicide.

Jack Johnson in Chicago, 1909.

Johnson strikes up the band in his Chicago Cafe Champion. He was often criticized for allowing both black and white patrons in his club.

Johnson and his manager, George Little (seated at left), close the deal for the Jeffries fight, July, 1910. Jeffries is seated on right.

Jack Johnson wanted to be paid off in gold and had to see it before the fight with Jeffries. His share was $30,000, here in $20 gold pieces. Tex Rickard, the promoter, is on Johnson's left.

Johnson and Jim Jeffries pose for the camera before the historic fight in Reno, 1910.

Jeffries, the retired heavyweight champion of the world, finds himself failing, even in the early rounds.

Jeffries uses the famous "crouch" which won him many bouts and the title from Bob Fitzsimmons in 1899.

Jeffries tried to connect a straight left to Johnson, but could do no damage to the solemn and impassive Negro champion.

Boxing critics believed that Jeffries could easily beat Johnson, but even Jeffries' strength failed to hold Johnson in the clinches.

Johnson ended the match in the fifteenth round with a knockout punch, thus defeating the retired champion.

Johnson and his third wife Lucille Cameron, outside his cafe in Tia Juana. They were married shortly after Lucille's mother charged Johnson with abduction.

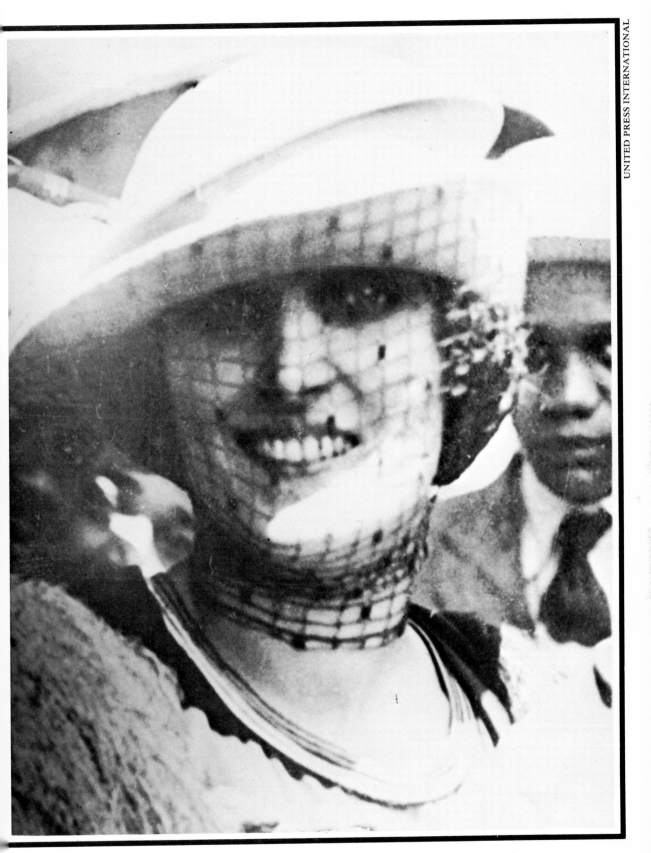

Lucille Cameron Johnson was working as a secretary in Chicago when she met Johnson. Before their divorce which ended 12 years of marriage, she accompanied Johnson on his world travels and saw him lose the heavyweight title in Havana.

Jess Willard, the "white hope of the people", downs Johnson in the 26th round in Havana, 1915. Johnson claimed he was shielding his eyes from the sun, but Willard won the title on the knockout count.

Johnson and his fourth wife, Irene Pineau, were married in 1925 when Johnson was 47 years old.

Johnson and his wife Irene introduce themselves at a night club opening in Chicago.

attended by an expression of public interest that almost overwhelmed me. I was the guest of honor at many celebrations indoor and out. A strong movement to arrange a fight for me in England was started and Bombadier Wells was tentatively selected as my opponent. He was willing enough to meet me, showing an admirable gameness, but it eventually was decided that he would in no wise be a match for me and negotiations for the fight were called off. Shortly after this, my party and myself set sail for home, arriving in the early part of January, 1911.

We returned to Chicago where I appeared in a series of theatrical engagements and other minor affairs. The field seemed to be entirely devoid of any contestants in the heavy-weight division. The cry for a "white hope" had subsided somewhat, though the hunt for such an antagonist had never ceased. Finding myself without ring opponents, I decided to open a cabaret and began completing my plans for the venture. As they proceeded, Jack Curley suggested a contest with Jim Flynn, whom I had met in 1907 in San Francisco and knocked out in eleven rounds.*

Flynn was a fighter of more than average ability. In my previous fight with him, I had recognized his high-class boxing talent. Since my defeat of Jeffries, Flynn had been doing considerable boxing and met some of the best of them. I felt that a contest between him and myself would prove an attractive one, and, furthermore, if he had championship timber in him I for one was as eager to find it out as any. The fight was arranged to take place in Las Vegas, New Mexico, July 4, 1912. Pending the fight and my training necessary for the event, I turned the plans for my cabaret over to others,

* Curley, an experienced promoter, persuaded Johnson to fight "Fireman" Jim Flynn, but the promotion failed and only 5000 people turned out for the match.

and again signed more theatrical contracts which kept me on tours up until the time for me to go into training. I established my camp at Las Vegas, having in my party as sparring partners and other assistants Calvin Respress, Watson Burns, Monte Cutler and George DeBray. During my training period Harry Wills appeared on the scene, seeking a place as sparring partner. I engaged him, but he remained only a few days. He proved wholly unable to stand the grind and was compelled to acknowledge that the ordeal was too much for him. He returned to New Orleans. The Flynn fight proved an easy victory for me and it also was the last I was to have on American soil for many years.

After the fight I returned to Chicago in readiness to open my Cabaret de Champion. During my absence at Las Vegas, its equipment, decorations and furnishings had been in competent hands and shortly after I arrived the opening took place. It was one of the most spectacular affairs ever held in Chicago, and I doubt if a similar event has ever taken place anywhere in the world. Friends came from all over the world to take part in the launching of the enterprise and when the initial opening of the doors took place, thousands of people struggled to gain entrance, and for hours afterward were lined up for many blocks, awaiting an opportunity to get within.

In the furnishing and decoration of the cabaret, I had spared no expense nor effort. Having traveled extensively, I had gained a comprehensive idea of decorative effects; I had viewed some of the most notable amusement centers of the world, both as to their exterior and interior arrangements. I also had collected many fine works of art, curios and novelties. These I used in providing the attractive features for which my cabaret gained considerable distinction. In addition, I had engaged artists and decorators of undisputed talents, whose ideas, combined with my own, resulted in an array of artistic creations which put to shame many similar establishments in both Europe and America—establishments which have attained world-wide prominence. In the art collection were paintings of myself and wife by a portrait artist who was rated as one of America's best. Other paintings were of my father and mother. I displayed a few real Rembrandts which I had obtained in Europe. Adorning the walls were original paintings representing Biblical and sacred history scenes. Another painting was of Cleopatra. These were only a few of the art subjects which adorned the walls of the Cabaret de Champion. There were numerous others, in all, the collection having represented a small fortune.

Other furnishings of the cabaret were on a similar plan. Only the very best of material had gone into the equipment. The bar tables and other pieces of furniture were of solid mahogany. Much of the woodwork, besides being of first class material, had been further improved by carving and polishing. The appearance of the interior was neither gaudy nor vulgar. I had striven to make it distinctive and attractive but also had combined with it real beauty and dignity. Another feature, and one which aroused much comment, and for which my cabaret was well known, was the silver cuspidors, decorated in gold. The opening night, as I have said, brought thousands, and it goes without saying that the occasion was a memorable one in Chicago. The celebration was one which will long be remembered.

The receipts that night were enormous. Money flowed plentifully and everyone enjoyed himself to the fullest extent. Throughout the entire existence of the cabaret it was successful financially and otherwise, and I sought at all times to conduct it, not only in accordance with the law, but with as good taste and as strictly as a business of that kind can be conducted. Naturally it attracted classes of people desiring lively times. All sorts of patrons came within its doors and there were those, of course, who would have caused difficulties wherever they went. Some of these frequently came to the Cabaret de Champion. Their conduct caused criticism, and this, in conjunction with the effort that was being exerted to put me in a bad light before the public, was seized upon to further my downfall. Prejudice also played a part, for in my cabaret the races had an opportunity to come in contact, a practice which in those days was not as well established as it is now. Unfounded rumors were afloat about my establishment which were easy to believe but hard to disprove. During my operation of the cabaret I did not attempt to fill any ring engagements. I was content to remain out of the spotlight of the ring and to give my attention to my business. Meanwhile there was a continual flow of criticism and condemnation and the insistent cry for the "white hope," was heard. I was perfectly willing that they should find a candidate, but I took no part in the discussion. When the tragic death of my wife took place I closed the cabaret and began directing my efforts in other channels. Naturally I gave considerable thought to future ring activities, but I had determined that I should conduct myself and my affairs in as quiet a manner as possible. I was tired of the public's consuming interest in me. However, the efforts of my enemies had not been lessened and when Miss Cameron's*association with me, of which I shall speak presently, presented the opportunity it did, they seized upon it with obvious eagerness. It turned out that instead of reaching a period of peace and quietness in life, I was in reality entering upon adventures that were to be more productive of public discussion and to embroil me in more adventurous exploits than ever yet had marked my life.

As recounted elsewhere, I was accused of violating statutory provisions and tried in the United States court. These accusations, my resistance to them, my trial and fight for my rights, occupied my attention for several months to the exclusion of either ring activities or other business affairs. During this time friends from many parts of the country rallied to my support and sought to aid me in the move to escape the unjust drive that was made upon me. The effort was unavailing, and in the desperation that followed I fled to Europe.

* Lucille Cameron became Johnson's third wife (his second white wife).

# CHAPTER V

## ROMANCES AND REGRETS

THERE have been countless women in my life. They have participated in my triumphs and suffered with me in my moments of disappointment. They have inspired me to attainment and they have balked me; they have caused me joy and they have heaped misery upon me; they have been faithful to the utmost and they have been faithless; they have praised and loved me and they have hated and denounced me. Always, a woman has swayed me—sometimes many have demanded my attention at the same moment.

Despite the rather devious and uncertain path I followed as a youth, my mother's splendid influence and love was never forgotten by me. I always loved her with the deepest affection. She would of course have had me select a different course in life from the one I did, but when that course was once selected and she realized that I was determined to follow it, because I believed it would lead to the success I desired, she stood back of me; she never wavered; she urged me to do my best. When others failed me she was my staunchest support; if others doubted me her faith grew the firmer. A good many reasons have been given as to why I attained a high place in the boxing world, but too little credit has been given to Tiny Johnson—my mother. It was she of whom I was thinking when I fled from Chicago to escape a prison term, and had she not expressed the wish that I should die rather than to become hemmed in by the stone and steel of prison walls and gates, it is probable that I would never have taken the desperate measures which I did. It was she of whom I thought when I wandered as an exile in foreign lands, and the longing to see her determined me to toss my freedom and my laurels as a boxer aside if necessary, to return to my native land. But she died before I could negotiate the return and while I was in distant lands, helpless to reach her, one of her last wishes was that she might see me. That was tragedy too, and a cause of heartache that has never left me.

I have three sisters, Lucy, Janie and Fannie and one brother, Henry. They have never figured publicly or prominently in my life. Lucy I must thank for propelling me into a youthful fistic encounter and making me fight when I was on the point of fleeing. Perhaps if I had never entered that particular fight I would not have learned that I really possessed fighting ability. It certainly instilled within me a courage that I never had previously experienced. I might say, therefore, that Lucy's determination on that occasion and the encouragement my mother gave me in after years were two very strong factors in pushing me to success.

As I approached manhood, it was the wish of my parents that I should marry, and in order to fulfil their desires, they went so far as to select the woman who was to become my wife. She was a young colored girl of excellent qualities, but I already had been smitten by the charms of another, a Galveston native whom I had long known. She was Mary Austin, and we were married in 1898, when I was twenty years old. Soon afterward I went to Denver and she accompanied me. My fortune in those days was somewhat lean, but we were devoted to each other and we were very happy. It seemed that noth-

71

ing would ever creep in to spoil our happiness, but it did. It started with a dispute of minor origin in Cripple Creek which caused her to leave me. Soon after, however, we were reconciled and together we went to the coast. But an invisible something gnawed at us which finally resulted in our permanent separation, which took place in Denver, in 1901. Mary was a splendid woman and I recall my life with her as one of the happy periods of my existence.

On my return from the coast following my fights with Kennedy, Jack Jeffries and others which I have recounted, and during my several ring engagements in Philadelphia, two other girls came into my life. They were Etta Reynolds and Clara Kerr. Both were colored girls and during my stay in Philadelphia I enjoyed their companionship and included them in my affairs as sources of great happiness. With Clara Kerr I became greatly infatuated. A deep attachment grew up between us which was to continue our association for a long time. When I returned to Chicago she came with me, and after a brief stay, during which I had some minor ring engagements, we went to California. My boxing engagements on this west coast trip were more successful financially and otherwise, and I was able to set up a splendidly furnished suite of rooms where we lived gaily and happily.

But this happiness was to have a maddening interruption. There had come to the coast a horse trainer with the Cornelius Vanderbilt string. His name was William Bryant, and I had known him in the early days of my New England life. I hailed him as an old and intimate friend and invited him to share our home with us. For a time the arrangement was a mutually satisfactory one, but suddenly just when I was congratulating myself on my success, taking the utmost pleasure in our home and being grateful for the presence of Clara in my life, she and Bryant ran away. Unknown to me, an attachment had developed between the two which resulted in their secret preparations to leave together. They took with them all my clothes, all other personal property of mine which was of any value, and disappeared one night when I was giving my attention to my ring affairs.

I was dumbfounded. For the second time a woman whom I greatly loved had fled from me, but this time the cause, instead of a trifling domestic dispute, was another man. The shock unnerved me. For the first time in my life my faith in friends and humanity had been shaken to the foundation. For a while I debated with myself as to what course I should take. Perhaps I should have let matters go as they were, but the more I thought it over the more I realized how much I esteemed Clara, and I determined that I would not let her get away from me. Having come to this resolve, I set about making inquiries and learned in which direction the couple had fled. Immediately I set out in pursuit. The trail led me to Tucson, Arizona, where I found them. I effected a reconciliation with Clara and we returned to Chicago.

Clara's flight had not only been a blow to my happiness, but it also had checked my earning activities, for I did not feel like returning to Los Angeles after what had happened, and it was there that some excellent opportunities were developing for me. On our return to Chicago our money was low and the boxing business was at a point which offered me few engagements. Consequently we were compelled to live modestly and to guard our savings which were going down rapidly. One day

I returned home and found Clara again missing. For a time I refused to believe the truth, but the emptiness of our home and the absence of her trunks and clothing together with what cash I had, convinced me that she had fled from me.

I began a search for her. My infatuation for her had never wavered. Throughout Chicago I wandered, making futile inquiries and eagerly tracing flimsy and useless clews. I could not find her or even learn in what direction she had gone. She had been swallowed up. The world became a void for me and for the first time in my life I succumbed to excessive drinking and other forms of dissipation. But I could not forget her and never for a moment did I cease the search for her. Finally, I became ill and so wretched in mind and body that I determined to leave the scene of my unhappiness and started eastward. I was without funds and was unable to borrow money, which caused me to believe that my friends had utterly deserted me, a frame of mind which, added to the turmoil I was in already, completed my state of discouragement. I made my way to Pittsburgh where I found some alleviation of my despair in the form of friends who realized my worries and unhappiness. They sympathized with me and sought to lift me out of my misery. They were liberal in their loans of money to me, but instead of using it judiciously I cast wisdom to the winds and gambled heavily. As a matter of fact I did not care what end I came to, for the thought of Clara and her disappearance was always uppermost in my mind.

At one period of my gambling activities I had prospered sufficiently to engage a drawing-room to New York, but before the train departed I lost every cent I had. I prepared to board the train penniless. A friend, Frank Sutton, knowing my predicament, insisted on lending me some money, but I refused to take it. Finally I did accept a dollar from him. Of this dollar I gave the train porter 50 cents; I bought two cigars with another quarter and the remaining quarter I tossed to a newsboy at the station when I arrived in New York. I had no plans in mind other than to continue the search for Clara. Somehow, I had a vague idea or hope that she might be in New York and that I would be fortunate enough to find her. I went to a boarding house kept by a woman with whom I was well acquainted and who with other friends in the city were liberal in helping me financially and otherwise to get on my feet. As I said I had no plans, but automatically I came in contact with the boxing and ring contenders and promoters. Fate was kind to me, and hardly without any efforts on my part matches were thrown my way in which I was not only successful in proving my boxing abilities but from which I netted more than $20,000 in less than a month. A few months previously this success would have elated me, but my love for Clara persisted and with it the desire to find her. Whenever opportunity offered I searched in the high and low places of New York for her, but without success. Eventually I gave up the quest and settled down grimly to training and boxing.

Other interests and other women helped to heal the wound Clara had caused, but she had not gone altogether out of my life. Several years afterward when I was happily married again I was shocked to read in the paper one morning that Clara had been arrested, charged with the murder of her brother. From the paper I learned that she was in prison at Tom's River, N. J., and that she was alone and friendless. I counseled with my wife who was familiar with Clara's presence in my life and together we went to the New Jersey Prison. We found Clara disconsolate in a prison cell. My wife went into the cell with her and did her best to cheer her up. In the meantime, I hunted up the district attorney with whom I discussed Clara's case. I employed lawyers for her and provided her with other funds and aid. She was acquitted of the murder charge and shortly afterward I helped her to acquire a small hotel which she has conducted successfully since.

The next woman who came into my life was Hattie McLay, a New York Irish girl. The heartaches which Mary Austin and Clara Kerr had caused me, led me to forswear colored women and to determine that my lot henceforth would be cast only with white women. At the time I met Hattie I was contemplating a trip to Europe and it was arranged that she should accompany me and aid me in looking after my business interests, which were assuming a more important volume than ever, because I was now determined to reach the Championship and was hot on the trail of Tommy Burns. This trip to Europe was financed by Hattie's father, and not by Sam Fitzpatrick, as most people were led to suppose. Fitzpatrick, while nominally my manager, did not invest much cash in the project and as far as his connection with me was concerned, merely carried out such plans as I made or directed.

Hattie was a splendid pal. She had good business judgment; she understood me, and our association for many months was a happy and prosperous one. She was destined to be with me on the occasions of some of my greatest triumphs in the ring, and to take part in many important and interesting events in my life. She accompanied me around the world on a trip that included every nation of consequence and several lesser countries and remote islands. She was in Sydney with me when I wrested the championship from Burns.

Our separation took place in Chicago and resulted from disputes that arose between us over her constant beer drinking. I remonstrated many times with her because of her penchant for beer which she drank to such excess as to cause me much embarrassment. In order to escape my detection when I sought to prevent her from obtaining beer, she smuggled the beverage into the house whenever opportunity offered, and I frequently found her much the worse for her indulgence and was mystified concerning the manner in which she obtained it. The secret was solved to some extent when one day I found numerous empty bottles hidden under her mattress which attracted my attention because of the bulging appearance of the bed. When my investigation revealed the presence of the many bottles, a final dispute took place and we separated.

About this time Belle Schreiber a Milwaukee girl of German descent attracted my attention and we became very good friends. It was she who was to appear later in my affairs as a factor involving me in legal difficulties, and who was to be an instrument in convicting me of charges which brought a prison sentence and my subsequent flight. However, Belle and I were happy together for a considerable length of time. She accompanied me to San Francisco when I went to fight Stanley Ketchel. This occasion was an embarrassing and disturbing one for me, because Hattie McLay also had gone to San Francisco. She had taken quarters in the same hotel and was intent on effecting a reconciliation with me. She watched the door of my room and sought many times to waylay me in the corridors. Naturally there was a state of warfare between Hattie and Belle which threatened to break out into open and disastrous hostilities any moment. While I was supposed to be complacently training for the Ketchel fight I was in reality in a state of turmoil and constantly was racking my wits to prevent an outbreak between the two women, and to avoid a scene between myself and Hattie. To avert this latter undesirable situation I was compelled to resort to many subterfuges. I slipped in and out of the hotel in a manner that would have aroused newspaper reporters to much excited speculation and would have provided many columns of gossip for the public's amusement, had they known of my maneuvers. My most successful method of leaving and entering my room was by means of a rope which I let down from a window when I was leaving, and which on my return was lowered to me when I signaled. It will be readily understood that I had a double reason for rejoicing when I had disposed of Ketchel and was ready to leave San Francisco, which I did with as little delay as possible. We returned to New York where I resumed my theatrical engagements and where not long afterward Belle and I separated and another romance came to an end.

After the Ketchel fight, I had quite a period of idleness as far as the ring was concerned, but was kept busy with my theatrical projects, having long contracts to fill. Much of my time was required in New York, and through my theatrical connections I met Etta Duryea, a Brooklyn girl of French-American extraction. This meeting resulted in our marriage in Pittsburgh in 1909.

She accompanied me on my theatrical tours in the United States and was a member of my party which toured Europe, it being my third trip across the Atlantic. This was primarily a pleasure party, but nevertheless I filled several music hall engagements, on request.

On our return to the United States, there were some more theatrical ventures, and then my fight with Jeffries, in Reno. Immediately after that fight, we returned to Chicago and opened my cabaret. The next few months were prosperous and happy. I felt that in Etta I had found a love that would continue uninterrupted, but in this I was sadly mistaken for it came to a tragic end when she committed suicide. I knew that she had been despondent, but attributed her mood to the death of her father which had taken place a short time before. Her father, a member of an excellent Brooklyn family, was greatly loved by Etta. There was between the father and daughter, an extraordinarily close attachment, and it was to be expected that his death would disturb her. However, I believed that her sorrow soon would pass and that she would resume her usual cheerful and happy disposition. Her attitude toward me had never changed. Our relations up to the last were joyful and peaceful. She never complained of anything and never gave any intimation that she was weary of life.

On the day that the end came, we had entertained some friends. Etta and I had arranged to accompany them to the train on which they were to leave the city. When the time came for their departure, my wife pleaded a headache, and begged that she be excused from going to the train. Her condition did not alarm me nor excite my suspicion. She said good-bye to our friends cheerfully and promised to meet them later. I went with them

79

to the train and when I returned home, I found the street in front of our apartment filled with crowds of people. Police wagons were drawn up and I experienced a chill that almost numbed me. When I arrived, friends told me to hurry upstairs that something had happened to Etta. Those ominous words gave me the worst fright I had ever had and I sped up the stairs, not knowing but dreading what I was to find. She lay on the floor, her beautiful long hair hiding her face. Near her was a revolver. On one exposed bare arm was a red spot. At the sight of it, I took courage and tried to convince myself that the shot had not been fatal. I gathered her up in my arms, and as I did so her hair fell back, revealing the ugly wound in her head. She died a few hours later.

This tragic event laid me low. It seemed that all I had attained was for naught. I closed the cabaret. I could not bear to think of continuing it, for she had been so significantly identified in planning and conducting it. I sought other channels in which to bury my disappointments and to find solace. For a time life palled on me. In the meantime, the hunt for the "white hope" went on and there were frequent rumors of possible contenders whom I should have to meet in defense of my title. I let matters drift and made no particular effort to interest myself either in business or in boxing.

Lucille Cameron, a Minnesota girl attending school in Chicago, was the next woman to venture within the circle of my activities. She first was introduced to me by Perry Bauer, and noting that I was distressed over business affairs, offered her services to straighten out my books. I employed her as a business secretary. Her association with me was purely of a business nature and devoid of undue intimacy. However, ugly rumors were in circulation and the public took them up eagerly. Attempts on my part to prove their untruthfulness were unavailing. One morning a newspaper reporter came to my home demanding to see Miss Cameron. I told him she did not make her home with me and directed him to the home of Jack Curley, where she was living, telling him he would find her there. Instead, he sent a telegram to her mother in Minnesota declaring that Miss Cameron was living with me. The result of this was to bring the mother to Chicago in a wild frame of mind. She came to my house denouncing and accusing me. I denied any improper association with her daughter, and, when she demanded to know where her daughter was, I offered to take her to her home. She accepted, and entered my car for the journey demanding that the curtains of the car be pulled down.

"Madame," said I, "everybody in Chicago knows this car. If they were to see it going along the street with the curtains down there would be such gossip and scandal that we would find ourselves in the midst of overwhelming censure. No, for your sake and for mine, I shall not pull these curtains down."

Mrs. Cameron was eager to see her daughter, and finally consented to ride with me with the curtains up. When we reached the home in which the daughter lived I took Mrs. Cameron in and summoned Miss Cameron.

"Lucille," I said, "your mother wishes to talk to you. Whatever she has to say to you will be for your good. Remember that she means more to you than any other person, and that whenever all others have failed you, your mother will stand by you. Whatever she wishes you to do will be for your welfare."

I left the mother and daughter together and made no effort to see Lucille again. The meeting between the mother and daughter was not satisfactory to the former, for she proceeded to have warrants sworn out for the arrest of both Lucille and myself. I was charged with abduction. Shortly after the arrest I was released on bonds, but Lucille was kept a prisoner in a hotel under the watchfulness of her mother and police. When I was tried on the abduction charge there was no evidence to support it and I was discharged. Countless other efforts were made to charge me with various crimes by Mrs. Cameron and others who were interested in the situation. On one occasion the late Charlie Erbstein, a well-known Chicago attorney employed by Mrs. Cameron, came to my apartment and I was forced to eject him because of his hostile attitude.

The search for the "white hope" not having been successful, prejudices were being piled up against me, and certain unfair persons, piqued because I was champion, decided that if they could not get me one way they would another, and all sorts of efforts were set in motion to brand me as an undesirable character and to relegate me to obscurity.

In the meantime, Lucille had escaped from the surveillance of her mother and the police and seeking me out begged me to marry her, declaring that she had been ruined in the eyes of the world, but that furthermore her mother was making her the object of abuse and nagging which she could not bear. She said that her home life never had been pleasant because she was held in check and not allowed such freedom as a girl of her age had a right to demand. I told her we could not marry, but that I would help her in every way I could.

She desired to leave Chicago and after thinking the situation over I decided that perhaps it would be best for all concerned if I arranged for her to go to Toronto, Ontario. She stayed but a short time and returning unexpectedly again begged me to marry her. I finally acceded to her wishes and we were married a short time afterward. This, however, did not bring an end to my troubles; they were only just beginning, for within a short time I was arrested on a charge of violating the Mann act.

My enemies, actuated by jealousies and prejudices had never ceased their activities. When they could find nothing involving me improperly with Miss Cameron, nor anything else in my record with which they could effect my downfall, they hit on an old trail, and learning of my association with Belle Schreiber, hunted her down. She was brought from Washington and set up as the accusing witness against me. Other witnesses were found willing to testify against me and so the case went to trial.

It was a rank frame-up. The charges were based upon a law that was not in effect at the time Belle and I had been together, and legally was not operative against me. The whole accusation was unfounded and I do not hesitate to say that fraudulent practices were adopted, so bitter and intense was the fight that had been opened up on me. I was sentenced to one year and a day in the penitentiary and fined $1,000. I appealed the case and the decision was reversed, but not until after I had taken flight and was beyond the reach of federal officials.

I am not one to defeat the ends of justice. Had I been

guilty of the charge which was hung over me, I would have taken my medicine and said no more about it, but I was stung by the injustice of the whole proceedings and hurt to the quick to think that the prejudices of my fellowmen and of my own countrymen, at that, could be so warped and so cruel. I went low in spirits. I was watched by a score of detectives, who, it appeared, believed that I was going to try an escape. At the first I had no intention of doing so, but it was maddening to be shadowed all the time. My car and my house were watched day and night. Every step I took was dogged. I was haunted every minute of my life and I must admit that it got on my nerves.

On one occasion my wife and I attempted to take a short vacation trip. Both of us were worn and worried. We went to Battle Creek, Michigan, and when the train reached the station in that city it was boarded by federal agents, and pounding at my state room door they demanded admittance. I told them that they could not come in—that Mrs. Johnson and I were not dressed. They insisted on entrance and for a moment I thought they were going to smash the door in. They waited, however, and donning our clothes we went out to meet them. They arrested me as a fugitive. They took me to the police station and the next day returned me to Chicago.

This incident increased the persecution from which I was suffering, and the desire to get away from it was born. I wished not only to throw the constant shadowing off my trail, but I wished also to put myself beyond the reach of the adverse publicity I was receiving. My character and life were being torn to pieces in the newspapers. Every day, on some pretext or another, my name was paraded before the public in glaring headlines. It was sickening—far worse than the prospect of the year in prison that awaited me.

To my mother, though, the prison was the principal source of worry; she was cut to the quick by the thought that I must enter prison, because after the manner in which I had been treated by my prosecutors, there was little reason to hope that the appeal would attain what I wished. I was harassed by the sight of my worrying mother as well as by the unhappiness of my wife and the shadowing of secret agents. My mother told me that she would rather that I die than that I go to prison. It was she who had furnished the bonds upon which I was at liberty. One night I told her I had planned a way of escape, but that if I departed I probably would never see her again, because it would mean exile for me from my native land. If I had hesitated previously in planning an escape or in carrying it out, all hesitancy came to an end when my mother begged me to go, declaring that she would prefer never seeing me again to having me spend a year in prison.

Friends, to whom I confided my intention of escaping, said that it was impossible. Some of them were alarmed over my determination to undertake the project. As I told them of my plans in part, I was within the sight, if not the hearing of secret service men. There was never a moment that they were not within reach of me. They hung close about my home and followed me every step through the streets, every time my car turned a wheel they were aware of it. To elude them did seem an impossible feat; yet I did.

There was in Chicago at that time a colored baseball team called Foster's Giants. I learned that the team had arranged for a game in New York City, and sending for the manager offered him and his team the use of a private car for which I would pay all the expenses to New York providing he would let me route the car. I did not tell him my purpose nor did he know that I was about to launch a daring move to throw off my shadowers and quit the United States. He accepted my offer with much expression of thanks.

Arrangements were made for the car, it was routed by way of Buffalo via New London. The ball team was composed of strapping big players, many of them as large as myself. One of the players resembled me in stature and features and to him I gave my watch and ring, the latter having more than once served as an identification of me, and being familiar to police and others when they gave my description. This was one of the ruses hit upon to serve in the event that officers, having got wind of my departure, boarded the train en route in search of me. The player resembling me, we believed, would be seized permitting me to continue my trip while he, as soon as the mistake had been discovered, would be released.

The ball team, Gus Rhodes, my nephew acting as my secretary and I, boarded the special car which had been arranged at Englewood Station. As the train pulled in, we stood in the shadows and when it stopped I, carrying a bag of bats and other baseball equipment, rushed with the rest to the car. The train immediately pulled out and I went to bed in the drawing room which I had reserved. The train sped on through the night; my flight had started, but how it was to terminate was a matter of conjecture. We were compelled to exercise the utmost caution. I was not disturbed until we crossed the Canadian border. At that point Canadian government officials came on board the train to inspect the baggage. All our baggage was placed outside the drawing-room and Rhodes stood by with the tickets informing the inspectors that the occupant of the room was ill and could not be disturbed. The explanation was satisfactory and they left the train.

At Hamilton, Ontario, we left the train on the blind side, Tom Flannigan, an old friend of mine, who had seen nearly all of my important fights, and who had attended every championship fight that took place during his life time, met us with an automobile and drove us to Toronto where Flannigan conducted a hotel. We arrived about four o'clock in the afternoon July 1, 1913, and Flannigan provided us with some cheese and ham sandwiches and a half dozen bottles of beer, a lunch after our all-day ride which I felt was the best I had ever eaten.

At Toronto I met my wife, who had left Chicago on a different train. We stayed in Toronto until late in the evening and then boarded another train for Montreal. We were on our way again. Neither I, nor anyone of my party, was recognized on the train until we arrived at Montreal, when a porter got a peep at me and soon broadcasted my presence in the city. That evening we were besieged by reporters and immigration officials. I gave a signed interview to the Montreal Star explaining the reasons for my trip. United States officials requested Montreal police to detain me as a fugitive, but upon it being shown that I had tickets good for passage from Chicago to Paris, France, and these placing us on bonds, as they did, Canadian officials could not hold me and, under the law, could do nothing but permit me to continue on my way.

We embarked at Montreal on the steamship Corinthia and arrived in Paris, July 10, 1913. We took up our quarters in the Hotel Grand in the Rue de St. Lazare where we remained for some time. When we arrived in the French port, a vast assembly of people awaited my arrival, among them numerous gendarmes, French police. When I saw them lined up intently watching the docking of our ship, I had a momentary feeling that my flight was to end disastrously, for I feared that some method had been devised which would enable my detention and I was hesitant about landing. But when I was informed that the gendarmes merely were a part of the crowd intent on giving me a warm welcome I experienced that well known grand and glorious feeling. Our reception at Paris was one of the most enthusiastic welcomes ever accorded me.

# CHAPTER VI

## Exile

IMMEDIATELY upon my arrival in Paris, I was offered several engagements in theaters and music halls.
Managers besought me on every hand, each trying to
outdo the other in offering me inducements. I decided
upon a short engagement at the Folies Bergére, where, as
long as I remained, crowded houses greeted me at every
performance. London music halls, too, were seeking contracts with me, and concluding my first contract in Paris,
I went to London and played for several weeks, bringing
my appearances there to a close when amusement promoters signed me up for a long contract which called for
my appearance at the leading amusement houses in
nearly all the capitals of Europe. The tour lasted several months, during which time I put on boxing exhibitions and other entertainments in Paris, Marseilles, Brus-
sels, Berlin, Vienna, Budapest, Bukharest, St. Petersburg, Moscow, and others of the larger cities of the old
world. Upon my appearance in each of these cities, I
was given a tremendous reception, large crowds meeting
me at the stations on my initial arrival and filling the
halls and theaters whenever I appeared. Ending the
tour in Vienna, I returned with my party to Paris where
negotiations had been under way for a match with Jim
Johnson, an American heavyweight.*

The fight took place in Paris, October 19, 1913. My opponent was a game fighter, and in the contest I, too, was
called upon to withstand one of the severest ring ordeals

* Jim Johnson was the first Negro Jack Johnson fought since winning the championship.

of my career, for in the third round my left arm was broken and I finished the fight with one arm, the broken one dangling helplessly at my side. However, I won the decision in the tenth round. The injuries I received in this battle made it necessary for me to devote considerable time to recuperation. With my arm broken there was little I could do in either stage or ring work, but I was not idle. My friends and I took advantage of the interruption to engage in sightseeing and touring which took us to most of the places of historic interest in France, and we enjoyed the experience hugely. I visited all the principal art galleries, nosed in and out of the quaint and picturesque quarters of Paris, made the acquaintance of many artists, writers and theatrical folk, and incidentally picked up some art works and curios which I added to my collection later.

When I was again able to engage in the strenuous work of boxing in stage exhibitions, I returned to London, where I had a long and successful music hall engagement which I closed upon the signing of articles for my fight with Frank Moran,* which took place in Paris the night of the Grand Prix, June 20, 1914. Because of the fact that my camp for training purposes was an outdoor one and the prevalence of exceedingly unpleasant and wet weather, I was unable to do much training and I entered the fight almost wholly unconditioned. Nevertheless members of my party and other fight authorities who had seen me in previous matches declared this was one of my greatest fights. Moran fought splendidly and I shall always remember it as an event of more than passing importance in my ring activities. We fought twenty rounds and I was given the decision.

After this fight there was considerable talk on the con-

* Francis Charles Moran, the Pittsburgh-born heavyweight.

tinent and in England of a fight between Sam Langford and me, either in London or Paris. This was a match that I should greatly have liked to see arranged. I had boxed Langford previously in America and had won over him in fifteen rounds. I had reason to believe, though, that the European fight would have been an interesting one, but it never came to a conclusion, owing to the lack of a promoter with sufficient finances.

On the failure of the Langford fight to take place, I resumed my theatrical appearances and had another successful London season at the end of which I decided to take my party to Moscow, establish headquarters and from that point tour Russia or such parts of it as offered encouragement for my exhibitions, or appealed to members of my party and myself for sight-seeing and touring.

On our way to Russia we encountered many troops. The movement of army detachments was a surprise to us. The trains were crowded with soldiers, and wherever we looked we saw cavalry, infantry and other units evidently under marching orders. There had been rumors of war in France and England for several weeks, but to these neither we nor others paid much attention. There seemed nothing serious about it. As we saw masses of soldiers moving in Russia, we recalled that while in France, during my training for the Moran fight we had seen troops maneuvering along the highways, but we did not give them more than a passing thought, merely supposing that it was a part of the regular routine of French military activity. In Berlin, several months before, we were impressed with the dominance of military life but thought it nothing more than a part of the German system of which we had heard much. There had been no thought of war such as was soon to prove so disastrous,

and change the geography of the world, but we were becoming more and more astounded at the hordes of soldiers about us, and I told my associates one day, when
I saw large bodies of troops training early in the morn-
ning, that war was brewing and that the whole of Europe
would be under powder smoke before long.

My predictions were fulfilled sooner than I had
expected. It was the first of July, 1914, when we arrived in Moscow. I had been negotiating several theatrical engagements and was awaiting the arrangement of
dates when war was declared. This put an end to amusement activities in all the countries concerned, and we
found ourselves not only beset on all sides by war preparations but very intimately concerned in Russia's side
of it, a situation having developed which brought me in
close contact with high Russian officials and agents.
There lived in Moscow a colored man named George
Thomas. He was a native of Georgia and when a young
man had left the States to seek his fortune. He became
a valet and when still a youth arrived in St. Petersburg,
now known as Leningrad. Thomas engaged in amusement enterprises throughout Russia and amassed a fortune. On our arrival, he was the owner of a huge
amusement park known as the Aquarium. It was a
veritable city, a city within a city; in it, besides its numerous amusement establishments and exhibitions were
residences, hotels, cafés, restaurants and other facilities.

Thomas and myself became close friends and we made
our headquarters in his park. As the war approached,
our host became engrossed in Russian war preparations,
for he was a factor of some importance in Russian political and commercial circles. He was a confidential
agent of Czar Nicholas, and I was greatly surprised to

learn that he was taking part in military councils and other phases of the war preparations. High military officers made their headquarters at hotels and restaurants in his park and it was while I, members of my party, and several army officers were dining together in one of these restaurants that we learned that war had become a reality. As we sat at the table some of my military friends were summoned to the telephone, told that war had been declared, and instructed immediately to join their units for hurried mobilization.

The country was in an uproar at once; the streets were filled with seething masses of civilians and soldiers. It seemed that every public place had been turned instantly into some kind of a military establishment. Telegraph and telephone messages were coming and going on every hand. Thomas, though not a military officer, was in the thick of it. He had been in Russia more than twenty years, and in that time had attained considerable power and authority. He confided much to me, and there probably were few foreign citizens in Russia who knew more of the inner workings of the military and political activities of Russia, during this period, than I. Thomas showed me many messages, some of which had been sent by the czar himself, which astounded me. Of a few of these messages I obtained possession, but they later were lost in the confusion that ensued. The contents of some of these would have made interesting and valuable data for historians or students engaged in analyzing the causes, factors and influences in the war, for they were personal exchanges between Czar Nicholas and the Kaiser, in which were discussed Russia's decision as to the part she would take in the conflict, the Kaiser urging the Czar to join with him in what he hinted would be a triumph which would enable Germany and Russia to rule the world. There were other messages concerning plans, attacks, defense measures and secret agreements, all pulsating with information, which, I realized afterward, were dangerous for a foreigner to possess.

Since theatrical engagements were out of the question with the great war launched, I concluded that Russia was no place for us, and that unless we got out immediately we might never be able to leave. The arrangement of transportation was no easy matter. Every device for travel had been seized for the conveying of troops. Furthermore, everyone was under suspicion and we had to give a strict account of ourselves. But for the aid of Thomas my party might have been prevented from leaving, and had that been the case we probably would have lost our lives, for vague information reaching me concerning Thomas was to the effect that because of his nearness to the Czar, he had to leave the country when the revolution came. He is now living in Constantinople.

We finally succeeded in starting the return journey to our home in Paris. We caught the last train to the border. At Warsaw we changed trains, which consumed much time. When we were finally placed in our compartment, I saw from the window huge piles of baggage, the loading of which apparently delayed our train. I therefore expressed the wish that they leave the baggage where it was and give their attention to moving the train. My wish was completely gratified for as we pulled out of the station I saw a truck-load of my own and my associates' baggage left behind on the platform. I regretted my wish and made frantic efforts to induce trainmen to stop long enough for our belongings, but there was no inducement I could offer which would move them to get the property, and on further investigation I found that instead of one truck being left we had lost three truck-loads.

On our arrival in Berlin, we found the city in turmoil and thousands of soldiers marching to the front. Excitement was intense. Vast crowds jammed the streets and it was almost impossible to make our way through them. We reached a hotel where we had arranged to have lunch, and here our party became somewhat embroiled in the war fever that was raging. In my party was a young Frenchman whom I had employed in my theater work. Recognizing his nationality, German waiters in our hotel began to taunt him. They told him that President Poincaré had been captured and was being held prisoner by the Germans. This enraged the Frenchman who shouted curses on the German waiters and hurled all sorts of epithets at them, causing a scene that for a moment threatened to involve us all in a miniature battle in the dining room. I managed to quiet the Frenchman and to make such explanations as would permit us to leave the dining room, and we hurried to our train.

Because of the rapid and heavy movement of troops and the eagerness of thousands of aliens to leave the country, trains were loaded with humanity. People crowded the aisles and packed themselves into every available space, some even hanging on at the risk of their lives outside the trains. Travel was in confusion; it was a nerve-racking undertaking. When we reached the Belgian border, we had to leave the train and complete the journey on foot to the first Belgian railway station. As diplomatic relations had been severed, no German trains were allowed to touch Belgian soil.

We did not remain long in Belgium, but went directly

to Paris where conditions were not much better. In Paris, we stopped only a few days. The whole attention and effort of the nation was turned upon the war, and, as the German troops advanced, the fear of invasion grew daily. Non-citizens, such as constituted my party, were in an embarrassing situation. There was no part which we could take in the war and little that we could do for ourselves. Facing these circumstances we disposed of our Paris household equipment and went to London. Here, too, was the war shadow, and every resource was being turned to the combat. But we were among English speaking people, and there was more calmness than in any of the countries we just had left. England was attempting to maintain amusements for her people and some of the music halls were open. I was invited to take another engagement in public entertainment, and did so, but gave it up on the arrival in London of Jack Curley, who came with a contract for me to sign providing for the meeting of Willard and myself in Juarez, Mexico, in a ring contest for my heavy-weight title.

Upon the signing of the contract I began preparations for the trip to Juarez. Gus Rhodes, my nephew, made a rather perilous and difficult trip back to Warsaw to obtain the baggage which we had been compelled to leave, and was successful in his mission. Despite the fact that our baggage had been retained for several months in the Russian station, Rhodes regained the entire collection, the only thing missing being a pair of shoes. In possession of our baggage again we settled up our affairs in Paris and London and started back across the Atlantic, our destination being Buenos Aires, where we landed Dec. 21, 1914.

# EXILE

The South American city gave me a rousing welcome and I was an object of much concern on the part of the people, all of whom treated me with the utmost kindness. I was immediately urged to fill some theatrical dates, and appeared in exhibitions in the capital and surrounding communities. In the meantime I engaged in an impromptu boxing match with Jack Murray, an American, who was traveling in South American countries meeting all comers. I made no preparations for the fight but succeeded in stopping Murray in five rounds. During my stay in Buenos Aires, I renewed acquaintanceship with Tex Rickard who had promoted my fight with Jeffries in 1910. He had temporarily retired from the promotion business and was engaged in raising cattle. Another American, Glen Cummings, joined my party in Buenos Aires. He was a young man of polished manners, highly educated and evidently from excellent family. He insisted on accompanying me, declaring that he had much money and was engaged in touring merely for pastime.

In the latter part of January, 1915, we obtained passage on a boat bound for the Barbados islands. It was not a passenger boat, being principally engaged in freight service, and I and my party, together with a few others, were the only ones on the boat excepting the crew. The trip was a wonderful experience and was enjoyed by all of us to the greatest extent, even though our engine broke down while we were on the ocean and we were confronted with the possibility of being cast adrift. Several days were passed without making any headway while the engine was being repaired and we took advantage of the delay to catch man-eating sharks which swarmed about our boat, many of which we hauled aboard. We eventu-

97

ally reached the Barbados none the worse for our experience with the disabled engine. We spent several days sightseeing and taking delight in the new scenes and customs with which we came in contact. In the meantime I was attempting to arrange passage to Havana, Cuba, but since there were not many passenger boats in service from the islands, and the fear of submarines and other ocean dangers created by the world-war caused most boats to hover near their home ports, it was difficult to find a way to make the trip. I negotiated with several owners of boats, the result on one occasion being a damage suit against me by one with whom I had had a misunderstanding of terms. In his suit he demanded a huge sum of money, evidently thinking me a man of large means and so eager to proceed on my way that I would pay without much resistance. But he was mistaken. I found that there were not many lawyers available—none at least whom I wished to act for me, so I went into court as my own attorney and surprised the judge and myself with my understanding of English law. I was able to hold my own against the lawyers prosecuting the suit against me, and on one or two points demonstrated that they were sadly lacking in their knowledge of the law. I won the suit and proceeded to charter the "Henry Craig," a small three-masted sailing affair, the owner of which I finally induced to brave the submarines and attempt to land us in Havana. When we left the Barbados a great farewell celebration was given in our honor. As our small craft left port, large crowds headed by leading personages of the port shouted adieus to us, and a band, which had played on the wharf as we prepared to embark, entered another boat and followed us several miles out to sea, playing all the way.

Our journey to Havana was a stormy one. We had been at sea only a day or so when we were caught in one of the fierce storms for which the Barbados region is noted. The gale swept us hard, and it seemed that our small boat would be demolished. Besides ourselves, there was not much of a crew aboard, there being only the captain, a boatswain, two colored deck hands, one able seaman and a Chinese cook. This crew had all it could do to keep the vessel afloat. Not only did we run into the teeth of one gale during the week, but several pounded down upon us, and there were several moments when we were certain that we were going to perish.

We battled the gale along the Havana coast for two days before we were able to make a landing. However, on February 15, we got into port, all of us thankful that we had escaped the death that seemed so certain. Cummings, the young American whom I had brought with me from Buenos Aires, accompanied us to Havana, but not until after he had involved us in some unpleasantness at the Barbados port, where he claimed that he had been robbed of a large sum of money by hotel employes. I made an effort to recover his money for him, but investigation proved that he had never had any money and that he was merely misrepresenting his financial connections. The manner in which he had duped me made me exceedingly angry, but there was nothing for me to do but bring him with me to Havana, for had I left him among the Barbados people, whom he had wrongfully accused, he would have paid dearly for his deception. As it was, I had a difficult time in saving him from their wrath.

Shortly before I left Buenos Aires, I had received information which made it necessary for me to balk on fighting Willard in Juarez. The proposed fight, while engineered by Jack Curley was being financed by Pancho Villa, the bandit leader who at that time had things much his own way in northern Mexico. Carranza, who was president of the republic, was, of course, not in sympathy with any move fostered by the revolutionary leader and he let it be known that he would stop the fight if he could. He had the means of stopping it, too, because I could not get into Mexico except by way of Vera Cruz. To have attempted entrance by any other port would have meant my capture and return to the United States, where the prison term awaited me. Carranza declared that if I attempted to land at Vera Cruz, he would make me a prisoner and turn me over to the United States. Confronted by this situation, I got in touch with Curley, who was at Juarez, and suggested that he arrange to have the fight at Havana. This change did not meet with Villa's endorsement and he withdrew his financial support. This, however, interrupted arrangements only temporarily. Frazee and Webber, well known American theatrical men were quite willing to take over the project, and in a short time all preparations for the fight were made and April 15, 1915, set as the date.

I started training, but facilities for my preliminary work were lacking and there were many other circumstances that prevented me from getting into first-class condition. On the day of the fight, my condition was fair and I could have defeated Willard and retained the title, but temptation had come to me and as I was stirred by the irresistible desire to see my mother, I was trying to decide upon a course that would enable me to return to the United States. I still was hesitant about entering prison, but at times had decided that I would return and serve my sentence for the sake of seeing my mother, but never got quite to that point. While I was in Europe I received word that my appeal from the judgment of the trial court had been successful. Although I was granted a new trial, I had put myself, by virtue of my flight, into the position of a fugitive from justice. Since I was absent from the country when the new trial was granted my original conviction stood and my bonds of $15,000 were forfeited. Preceding the Willard fight it was hinted to me in terms which I could not mistake, that if I permitted Willard to win, which would give him the title, much of the prejudice against me would be wiped out. Those who chafed under the disappointment of having a man of my race hold the championship, I was told, would be mollified, and it would be easier to have the charges against me dropped, and I could again be with my folks.

It was no easy decision. It meant the sacrifice of my heavy-weight title which I had striven years to attain, and which had brought me so much; it would brand me as a quitter and as unsportsmanlike and would, I knew, relegate me to an undesirable position in sport circles. On the other hand, there was held out the hope of returning home to those who were dear to me, and the possibility of finding leniency on the part of federal officials. There was the chance that I would not be imprisoned; that there would be no further prosecution of me, and that I might settle down quietly and live in peace with my fellow-men.

As I trained for the fight, these thoughts were uppermost in my mind. Day after day I reviewed the situation and the future possibilities. I did not cherish the championship title so much that I was willing to sacrifice

the companionship of my mother nor peace and contentment and an opportunity to live in the country I loved so
much, even though I had fled from it. Yet, if I gave up
the title, I would be assailed as unscrupulous. My mind
was in a turmoil. It was necessary for me of course
to use some mental energy in my clash with Willard.
From all sides of the ring I was being jeered and taunted,
and I could not refrain from flinging back hot replies
that seethed up in my disturbed mind. However, in spite
of this mental struggle, I felt all the way through that
I was mastering Willard. I could have disposed of him
long before the final round.

Willard was declared the new champion. I came out
of the ring officially the loser, but not suffering the disappointment of defeat, because I believed that I had done
that which would enable me to return home and with the
prejudices against me somewhat removed. My future
would be devoid of the antagonism that constantly arose
over my holding the championship title. As matters
turned out, I had cause to regret my action, for after I
had permitted the title to pass to Willard, I found that
such offers or hints of leniency as had been tendered me
were without substantial foundation, and that immediate
prospects for my return to my own country without going to prison were so slight that I could not give them
serious thought.

This realization brought upon me bitter disappointment, more intense than if I had lost the championship
at the hands of a man who was my superior. The sacrifice I had made was of no avail. I could not return
home and the high hopes that I had entertained at the
thought of soon seeing my mother, vanished. I still was
to be a wanderer and hunt my haven in a foreign country.

I remained a short time in Cuba after the fight, and then began arrangement of my affairs in order to permit my return to England. In the meantime, Rhodes, my secretary, and all members of my party who had traveled with me from Europe to Buenos Aires and Havana, with the exception of Mrs. Johnson returned to their American homes.

This was a heart-breaking experience for me and for a while I was in exceedingly low spirits. I had many friends in Cuba and they remained steadfastly by me in these disappointing hours. Having failed in their efforts to aid me in returning home, they united their efforts to promote my welfare and make my life more pleasant. Among these friends was General Mario Menocal, who was then president of Cuba and who had taken great interest in me and the fight. He had visited me in my training quarters, and after the contest renewed his friendship by showering me with many kindnesses and courtesies. His children and I had become great friends and to them I gave the medicine ball which had been part of my training equipment.

From Havana Mrs. Johnson and I returned to London and I gave my attention to the organization of a musical review, which I designated "Seconds Out." I engaged the best stage talent available in London, and after a successful period in the city with the production which attracted crowded houses at all performances, we took the organization on the road and filled dates in all the principal cities of England, receiving everywhere a welcome and patronage that was gratifying and profitable. We continued the show until January, 1916, when we closed it, having been tendered inducements by theatrical promoters in Spain which prompted us to go to that country. In the review, I took one of the leading speaking parts, in addition to engaging in boxing exhibitions. In these parts I feel that I acquitted myself successfully. Newspaper accounts of my efforts as an actor were highly favorable, and the capacity houses which greeted us were ample evidence that the review met with public approval.

San Diego was the first Spanish city in which I and my party made the acquaintance of Alfonso's subjects. Here, as in every other European city which I visited, I was given an enthusiastic reception. Large crowds met us as we landed and followed us cheering as we went to our hotel. From San Diego we went to Madrid where pleasant and profitable circumstances occasioned our stay for several months. I engaged in several theatrical performances and minor ring bouts, the latter being principally exhibitions between myself and members of my party. There are few boxers in Spain and there were none at that time whose ability was sufficient to warrant serious bouts with me. The Spanish, however, take keen delight in watching a boxing contest, though they declare that it is not a sport equal to bull fighting, and consider it rather odd that a man finds enjoyment in being knocked about by another.

From Madrid I went to Barcelona, a city with which I at once developed a happy acquaintance. It appealed to me more than any other European city and I decided at one time that I would make it my permanent home, and with this in view, went so far as to purchase a house in which to settle down. At about this time I also began to consider establishing myself in some other business and looked around for opportunities outside the theater and boxing ring. The result of this was the establishment by myself of an advertising agency. Advertising was a profession which had attracted me to a considerable extent, and one which I understood quite well because of my extensive use of publicity in the theatrical and boxing world. I did not reckon with the fact, however, that Barcelona was a city which still harks back to ancient methods of doing business and my undertaking was not a very flourishing one. Clients were unaccustomed to making use of such an institution and so my venture, while not altogether a failure, was not as successful as I could have wished. The ring and theater continued to appeal to me and I returned to the stage, repeating some of the performances which had won success elsewhere across the Atlantic. I also arranged a ring contest with Arthur Craven*who was an English heavyweight and had fled to Spain because of the war. A large crowd was attracted by the contest which lasted but a short time, for I knocked him out in the first round.

By this time I had become well known in Spain and frequently was urged to make public appearances. Bull fighting being the most popular sport of that country, I naturally took much interest in it and was a frequent visitor at these events. Whenever I appeared in the stands a demonstration took place which was almost equal to that accorded the matadors or bull fighters themselves, who are national heroes to the people of Spain. As my interest increased in the Spanish sport I cultivated the acquaintance of many matadors among whom were Joselito and Belmonte, who at that time were ranked as the greatest matadors of the country. Both these champions had been interested spectators at boxing and theatrical presentations in which I had taken part. They professed much admiration for my strength and speed

* Arthur Craven (Fabian Avernus Lloyd), twenty-nine years old at the time of the bout, was well-known for his poetry and travels in bohemian circles. A year after the fight with Johnson, Craven disappeared, and though reports of his death were widely circulated, his body was never found.

and planted the seed of a new ambition within me when they declared that I would make a splendid success in the bull ring.

I determined to acquire the art of the matador. My friends Joselito and Belmonte were delighted, and eagerly undertook to instruct me. I was an enthusiastic and apt pupil and they were willing and efficient teachers. We made rapid progress and it was not a great while until they pronounced me competent for a public appearance, and so on July 10, 1916, I appeared in the arena wearing the picturesque costume of the bull-fighter. All Barcelona turned out to see the pugilist turned matador. Squeezed into the tight-fitting trousers which constitute a part of the matador's garb, to say nothing of the flaring cape, I did not feel as comfortable as when appearing in the scant attire of the boxer. I awaited with anxiety the appearance of the bull which I was to fight.

I was confident of the outcome, because having drawn lots earlier in the day for the bulls that we were to fight, there had fallen to me an antagonist of small size, and I believed I could handle him easily. I was due for a shock, for when the gates swung open there came tearing forth a monster bull. I thought he was as high as a house; he was an angry, snorting creature, too, and it appeared that the sensible thing for me to do was to let him have the arena to himself. I was quite willing to show how speedy I was in a demonstration of how to get out of a bull ring, but in this I was hindered by my tight-fitting trousers and the further circumstance that there were vast throngs of humanity in the stands, through which it would be impossible for me to flee even if I could, by some mysterious process, have flown over the high walls of the arena. The only thing I could do was to stand my ground. I met the bull in his onrushes in accordance with the recognized customs of the best matadors. I found that the huge bull, though much slower than a skillful boxer, nevertheless was equipped with many clever tricks, and that I could not side-step him as I could the fist of a boxer. At any rate I was the victor. I delivered the fatal sword thrust at the proper time and in a manner that won for me the plaudits of the crowd. I killed three bulls on the occasion of my first appearance in the Spanish arena, and at the conclusion of the performance found that I was almost as much of a favorite as their beloved champions. I took part in other bull fighting contests and gained considerable fame. My matador friends predicted a successful future for me as a bull ring attraction, but the sport did not find high favor with me, because I preferred to return to the cushioned gloves.

My experiences in the bull ring had increased my popularity in Spain and, when I returned to theatrical work in which I appeared in several boxing exhibitions with Rhodes as my partner, I had the satisfaction of drawing large houses. I believe that my stay in Spain had the effect of creating a new interest in boxing in that country, for several efforts were made to arrange ring contests for me by Spanish promoters which efforts failed only because none could be found to engage in ring battles with me. However, I did succeed in arranging one event, my antagonist being an American named Blink McCluskey, who hailed from Philadelphia. On the night of the fight McCluskey came near precipitating a grand failure by refusing to enter the ring unless he received a greater percentage of the proceeds, his change of front taking place when he saw a house crowded to its fullest capacity, and realizing that the proceeds were to be much in excess of what he at first had expected. He held out for a long time delaying the contest, and causing the spectators to grow uneasy. The dispute and delay he had occasioned so angered me that when we did enter the ring I was in a worse temper than I had ever evidenced in the meeting of a boxer, and I proceeded to give him one of the worst beatings I had ever forced upon an antagonist, and knocked him out in five rounds.

Boxing, theatrical engagements, advertising and bull fighting did not include all my activities while in Spain. When the United States entered the war, I found an opportunity to serve the country from which I was a fugitive by conducting investigations of German submarine operations off the coast of Spain, and I also engaged in wrestling matches, in one of which I defeated the Castilian champion.

In my work as an American agent, I was employed by the American military attaché in Spain, Major Lang, and pursued my assignments under the direction of the intelligence department. At that time, German submarines were causing havoc with English and American shipping. The destructive boats were appearing as if by magic in numerous places on the sea. They were baffling allied naval experts by the suddenness with which they did their damage and the mysterious manner in which they disappeared. It was evident that they had bases somewhere on the west coast of Europe, or had devised hiding places so near the scene of their depredations that they constituted the greatest menace to the successful prosecution of the war by the allies. Feeling sure that the sub bases, or at least some of them, were on the

Spanish coast, I was sent out to discover what I could.

I made no pretentions to military training nor had I any experience as a sailor, but the accumulated experiences of my life-time served me well in these ventures, to which were attached numerous risks including the traversing of rough water into dangerous and out-of-the-way places along the coast, infested not only by possible war enemies but by smugglers and others engaged in outlaw practices. Then, too, there was the danger of capture by the enemy and the possibility of death by promiscuous shooting which frequently took place between the furtive craft in those waters. I was in and out of various sea ports and spent considerable time at San Sebastian and San Tandier and visited several islands off the coast. I obtained much information which was of sufficient value to be communicated to the United States officials who in turn submitted it to the allies for use in resisting submarine warfare and safeguarding shipping. For my work and the information which I obtained I received due recognition from the officials under whose instructions I operated, and I had the great satisfaction of being of service to my native country, even though I was an exile.

In undertaking wrestling bouts, reference to which I made a moment ago, I found similar limitations as existed in finding boxers in my division. Wrestling in Spain, like boxing must take a secondary place to bull fighting, as a result of which there are not many skilled in the former type of athletic sport. However, Spain boasted of one wrestling champion in the person of Juan Ochoa, and with him a match was arranged for me. We met about the middle of July, 1918. The scene of our encounter was the bull fighting arena at Bilbao.

It was on a holiday and festival gaiety reigned. Great crowds packed the stands and cheered the contest which was not a difficult one for me, for I took the champion for a fall in eighteen minutes.

While I am making reference to my wrestling matches in Europe, I must retrace my steps a little to a time before the outbreak of the war when I was meeting all comers in the boxing arena and was engaged in theatrical productions in France. A wrestling tournament of considerable magnitude was being promoted in Paris, and I was one of the entrants. I met several opponents and found none who were my superiors on the mat. I met both French and German twisters, and on one occasion I was billed to meet one of the latter nationality. He came recommended as a skillful wrestler and also a dangerous and tricky one. The latter quality I found he possessed to excess. He began the use of fouling tactics from the beginning. I bore his unfairness for some time, but, when he was encouraged by my patience to apply his out-ruled methods more and more vigorously, I resorted to boxing habits and applied a blow to his jaw which knocked him out. This feature of the bout was more appreciated by the spectators than any other match on the program. When it was realized how I had terminated the struggle there was a burst of cheering from that French audience that astounded me. I found out later that they were not cheering because an unfair combatant had been punished, but because he was a German.

Another wrestling event in which I took part was in Sweden, when I made a tour of that country, of Norway and of Denmark. At this time I beat Hansen, who was the wrestling idol of that country. Our meeting took place at Gothenburg, and the outcome was a surprise to the wrestling fans who believed Hansen unbeatable. However, they took his defeat in sportsman-like manner and treated me with the utmost kindness and respect.

Early in 1919 I received overtures from boxing promoters in Mexico City, who opened negotiations with me to visit that country for the purpose of getting me to appear in a series of boxing matches. After considerable correspondence two of the promoters visited me in Madrid, and it was arranged that I should leave Spain where I spent four years. But for the fact that I was compelled to forego the pleasure of returning to my own country where I had been treated with less kindness than anywhere in the world, my years in Spain would have been happy ones. As it was I was haunted by the constant wish to see my own country and to live amid the scenes that were dearest of all to me, and the unpleasant prospect of a prison term hanging over me. Then there was the added bitterness that my mother had died when I was hopelessly beyond her reach. Her death had occurred in March, 1917, and after that time I felt so much uneasiness that it was difficult for me to decide upon a definite course, yet never did the desire to return to America leave me. I accepted the opportunity to go to Mexico City, with deep satisfaction, because it would bring me nearer home and might be an important step in ultimately ending my exile one way or another. I sailed from Spain March 28, 1919. Rhodes did not accompany me, but went to New York City to make arrangements for sending boxers to Mexico City for the ring series we were contemplating. In the meantime he visited Chicago and did not join me in Mexico until the latter part of July. Marty Cutler, George DeBray and Jack Heinan with whom Rhodes had signed contracts preceded him to Mexico City, and the matches were well under way when he arrived. In these fights I was the principal boxer appearing in a great number of bouts with both visiting and native combatants and winning in every contest.

In Mexico City I made many friends among whom was Carranza, who at that time was the president of the republic. When initial negotiations for my fight with Willard were under way and Villa, the bandit chief, had promised to finance the meeting in Juarez, Carranza showed his disapproval by threatening to arrest me for the United States authorities in the event I attempted to land in Vera Cruz, which, it will be remembered, caused the fight to be staged in Havana. Soon after my arrival in Mexico City from Spain, Carranza tendered me his friendship and made every effort to make my stay in the Mexican Republic a pleasant and comfortable one, even going so far as to provide me with escorts of soldiers when I had occasion to travel in sections of the country infested by bandits or revolutionists. The president also took much interest in our ring exhibitions and frequently we met each other in private, at which times we engaged in conversations which ranged over many subjects. Carranza was a man of broad views, was well educated and despite the uncertain political situations which he faced—situations which sometimes held the threat of death for him and the overthrow of his government—he found time and the inclination to give his attention to the consideration of many things which did not pertain to his personal success. He was greatly interested in world politics and in the future relations between his country and the United States. He questioned me concerning my experiences in Europe and drew from

me my views on international politics, which, although I
was by no means an authority upon the subject, he
seemed to believe were worth listening to.  To be sure, I
had in the years of my residence in European capitals
gathered much information along the lines in which he
was interested, and he lost no opportunity to encourage
my expressions of opinion.

Following my bull fights in Spain, I had determined
not to engage further in contests of this nature, but
rather to devote myself intensely to my boxing, but my
friends and others in Mexico City, having learned of my
experience as a matador in Barcelona and other Spanish
cities, frequently urged me to enter some of the contests in Mexico, where of course bull-fighting is quite as
popular as in Spain.  I was in no particular mood to de-
viate from my course as a boxer.  However, I had discussed bull-fighting considerably and even had gone so
far as to write newspaper articles on bull-fighting, which
seemed to establish me in the minds of the public as an
authority. My hesitancy in again pitting myself against
bulls only increased the ardor with which my Mexican
friends insisted upon my donning the colorful costume of
a matador, with the result that I took part in some of
the bull-fighting exhibitions which were being frequently
held in Mexico City and vicinity.  I had no difficulty
in these events and won considerable popularity among
the fans, who, like friends in Spain, sought to induce me
to make this form of sport my profession. But, although
it is one of the world's greatest sports in my opinion, and
calls for much courage and skill, it does not hold for me
the inducements that boxing does, and after several contests with the sword and cape as my weapons, I again
turned my attention to ring activities.  The boxing

series, which had been the object of my trip to Mexico, was in the main successful, but it was difficult for me to find opponents and there were long stretches of time during which I was idle.

At about this time too General Obregon was actively engaged in fomenting revolution against the Carranza government, and conditions in the Mexican capital and other parts of the country for that matter were none too pleasant for Americans or other foreigners. I began, therefore, to plan for other activities. I had been urged by the governor of Lower California to visit that section where he was interested in seeing the successful promotion of boxing events in the belief, I presume, that it would prove an added attraction for tourists. He offered such inducements that I determined to change my base of operations and, accordingly, set out for Tia Juana, a journey that proved to be fraught with many hardships and dangers, and one which nearly claimed the lives of myself, Mrs. Johnson and Rhodes. An American family which had been living in Mexico City joined us in our departure, having been compelled to leave because of the activities of the revolutionists. Ordinarily, the trip would not have been a severe one, but owing to the relations that existed between myself and United States authorities, it was not practicable for me to make the trip in the customary manner which would have necessitated going to El Paso. For this reason, it was necessary for us to travel in a round about way, our course running through Guadalajara and Sonora, two Mexican states in which bandits, as well as Indian tribes, were indulging in depredations. Trains were running irregularly in this section of the country. They were being held up daily, and in many instances wrecked. Passengers

114

were robbed and many were slain. These conditions were not inviting, but we determined to face them. Because of interrupted train service and the lack of railway facilities in some instances, part of our journey was accomplished with mules, which we rode or which pulled us over the rough roads in crude springless vehicles which were worse than the backs of the mules.

On one occasion, in Sonora, our train was stopped by a horde of savage Yaqui Indians who were supposed to be in sympathy with the revolutionary movement, but, in reality, used this principally as an excuse for pillaging trains. They were none too gentle in their methods. They did not hesitate to kill on the slightest provocation and the charred embers of what once had been railway coaches, which were scattered along the rail line were mute evidence of the lengths to which they had gone in carrying out their raids. When our train was stopped, passengers were driven from the coaches, and our assailants proceeded to search them. Some busied themselves with the baggage, and were engaged in tossing all of the passengers' possessions through doors and windows. I alighted from the train with the others and as the Indian bandits began their indignities, I began talking to them, having gained sufficient knowledge of the Mexican vernacular to make them understand. When I told them who I was, they were sufficiently interested to halt their looting, and came trooping about me, their curiosity overcoming their interest in their work of robbery. At first, they doubted that I was actually Jack Johnson. I had no idea, however, that they had ever heard of me, for I did not expect that these savages had much knowledge of what was going on in the world. I was surprised to find that they did know who I was, and for a moment, when they were convinced of my identity, it appeared that they were going to stage a wild demonstration in my honor. They manifested more interest and excitement over my appearance than they had in the promise of loot. Leaders of the band were profuse in their apologies for molesting the train, declaring that had they known I was aboard, they would not have thought of stopping the engine. What loot they had taken they restored to the passengers and told us that we might go on. I mingled freely with the Yaquis and when our train pulled out they were in a most friendly mood. I later was heaped with thanks by the passengers who had good reason to believe that had the Indians carried out their original intentions, they might not have lived to relate their experiences.

Having reached Sonora, we cut across the country westward to the Lower California coast. We found our way to Mazatlan, a small port where we sought to arrange passage northward. There were not many boats of any description sailing the route which it was necessary for us to take, and it was a difficult matter for us. Finally I came in contact with the captain of a small gasoline driven launch, who said he would undertake to carry us to our destination. The launch was nothing more or less than one used in the business of smuggling Chinese across the border into the United States, and when we went aboard we found that as fellow-passengers we were to have about 50 Chinese recently arrived from the Orient, and of a type not particularly inviting as associates. Besides them and the captain there was one deck hand and a cook. Mrs. Johnson was the only woman aboard and had she been less plucky, she would have shrunk in fear from joining such an expedition. The first day of our voyage was pleasant and smooth enough, but before midnight we ran into a storm that picked up our small launch and tossed it about so violently that we believed our escape impossible. The captain had been engaged in navigating along this particular stretch of water for twenty-five years and was well acquainted with the coast. Knowing of sheltered strips of water, he managed to turn the launch toward shore and succeeded in nosing it into a small bay in which we were free from the dangers of the storm. Here we remained the rest of the night and until late in the afternoon of the following day while the gale on the gulf continued to rage. We were glad enough to go ashore from the launch when daylight came, because we had had an experience that had racked our nerves. However, when we were on shore we found that we were in a desolate, barren and apparently uninhabited section of the country, but as we explored further inland, we discovered that it was not uninhabited, but that it was the camping place of a tribe of Indians, the name of which I never learned. Perhaps they had never acquired any designation for they were without doubt the lowest in the human scale that I had ever seen. They had human forms but other than that they were animals. They were even worse than animals for I have never seen animals so unclean and so lazy as they were. They were naked and their skins were filthy with slime. They lay about their camps like vermin, men, women and babies piled up together with dogs who had the same privileges as the others—privileges which permitted them to nurse at the breasts of the human mothers who lolled listlessly about, a suckling babe on one side, a dog on the other. These Indians, I was told, were of a ferocious nature and had attacked strangers who had ventured among them previously; but we were not molested by them, and because of their filthiness, we did not remain near them long.

In the afternoon the storm abated, and the gulf waters appeared to be quiet enough for us to resume our voyage. We left our sheltered spot and took to the open again. Scarcely had we reached the gulf proper when another gale struck us. It was more intense than the one from which we had fled on the day before. The waves rolled upon us mountain high and were gigantic enough to swallow boats, much larger than our own. The launch was tossed from the crest of one wave to another with as much ease as a couple of stalwart athletes throw a football about. The wind blew at a terrific speed and threatened to strip the launch of every shred which it bore and suck its human freight down into the surging waters. The captain sought to turn about for the coast again, but was unable to do so. The storm was so furious that his only possible means of safety was to keep the nose of the craft straight ahead. To attempt to turn meant that it would be dragged down. Assailed by the roaring winds and the tumultuous water, we found ourselves headed for the open sea. The storm raged for hours. Our captain said it was the worst he had ever encountered in all his years in those waters. I do not hesitate to say that I was frightened; both Rhodes and myself concluding that this would be our last earthly venture. The Chinese passengers were panic stricken with fear and the captain, though determinedly battling for the safety of his craft, declared more than once that we were lost. There was nothing any of us could do either in navigating the launch or adopting some means of safety. We were helpless and every minute we expected would be our last. In all this tumult of water and wind and human fear, Mrs. Johnson was the calmest one aboard. I never knew such gameness in man or woman. The storm continued the better part of two days and every minute of those two days was one of agony. Wave after wave rolled up and against us; the wind howled about us, slapping the launch about as it pleased, and tore furiously at the water.

How that little craft survived I do not know, but it did. When the storm subsided, we were many miles out of our course. As soon as the wind and water quieted we tacked about and eventually were on our way again, but at no time did the gulf become smooth. We had a constant battle with the rough waters and were never out of danger until we reached the Colorado river, into which the launch was steered. I have never experienced a moment of greater relief than I did when, for the first time after several days, I realized that we were safe. I was more or less astounded to find that we were out of danger, for when I thought of the raging wind and water through which we had come I was unable to understand how, with such a frail craft, we had escaped.

We chucked along up the Colorado river for a day or more, when we reached an isolated landing, without a name, as far as I could determine. It was at this landing that the smuggled Chinese left the boat, hiking from there for many miles to the Texas border where at an equally isolated spot they crosed into the United States. At this landing, we were compelled to lay-to for several hours awaiting rising of the river tide, so that we could continue our journey. During the wait, we decided to go ashore because we were stiff and sore as a result of our long stay on the boat and the terrific knocking about which we had suffered. We effected the landing and began to explore about, rejoicing in the good fortune and the thrill of touching land again. Our happiness, though, was to be short lived for within a short time after leaving the boat, and as we were busying ourselves with the things of interest about us, a regrettable accident occurred, when a gun which I carried was accidentally discharged, the bullet striking Rhodes in the arm. It caused a serious wound. There was no doctor at hand and no other facility for giving him aid. Tia Juana was 150 miles distant. We were unable to float our launch and delay was dangerous. The only thing for us to do in an effort to obtain the necessary aid for Rhodes was to start the trip to Tia Juana overland, and we lost no time in setting out with the wounded man. I had succeeded in getting a message to a telephone and over that I had sent a call to Tia Juana for an automobile. In the meantime, Rhodes lay in an abandoned cabin. Upon the arrival of the auto Rhodes was rushed to a hospital at Mexicali, where he lay several weeks but where he made a successful recovery, joining me at Tia Juana. The drive across the desert with Rhodes was a nerve-racking experience. The patient with a gaping wound in his arm suffered tortures, but he showed remarkable courage, without which he doubtless would have died from loss of blood and lack of attention which, though we were eager to give, was impossible.

As soon as I reached Tia Juana, I found that several bouts had been arranged for me. The sportsmen, tourists and others apprised of my coming awaited me anxiously and gave me quite a welcome on my arrival.

In spite of the gruelling experiences through which I had been—the storm at sea, and the drive across the desert with the injured Rhodes—I was in excellent physical condition, and lost no time in taking on several boxers who had been engaged to meet me. There were none, however, in the group who proved difficult as antagonists and the bouts were of so little importance that they do not merit description, though I may add that I won all of them easily. Boxing in Tia Juana served only temporarily to occupy my time and attention. It was not a profitable occupation and I sought other means of assuring my income.

Soon I opened a café, which was popular from the start and well patronized by visitors from the States and other parts of the world who were flocking into Tia Juana because of the lack of restrictions prevailing at that time. But I was not satisfied with my lot in life. There was nothing, I felt, which would compensate me for continuing as an exile from my home and friends, so I thought constantly of returning but was at a loss as to how I should proceed.

While this question was uppermost in my mind, after a stay of six months or so in Tia Juana, Tom Carey, a well known Chicago politician and one time candidate for Mayor of Chicago, and for many years a close friend, arrived in Tia Juana to visit the races. We were not long in renewing our oldtime acquaintance, when I picked six winning horses for him out of seven races. During his stay we spent much time together and visited most of the places of interest. During our association I confided to him my wish to return to the United States and discussed with him the difficulties which confronted me. He understood my wishes, and insisted that I should return, offering his service both as a bondsman and mediator, promising to make the way for my return as easy and generally satisfactory as he could. With the assurance of his good offices, I decided to surrender myself, and communicated with the Sheriff of Los Angeles county and federal officials, telling them that I wished to cross the border into the United States. I was instructed to go to San Diego where the proper officials met me, and where I arrived after surrendering the passports of myself, Mrs. Johnson and Rhodes. I was back on American soil again and the realization thrilled me quite as much as though I were entering the realms of a strange and unexplored land. I was filled with the thoughts of again seeing loved and familiar faces and of walking among scenes that were old and dear in my memory. There were many formalities to be disposed of before I could begin the journey to Chicago—a journey which I anticipated with more eagerness than any journey which ever before I had contemplated even in the most enthusiastic days of my youth.

# CHAPTER VII

## The World Through Prison Bars

IT was arranged that I should make the trip to Chicago virtually as a free man. Carey and Rhodes had preceded me, and were making preparations for my arrival when I left San Diego. Newspapers all over the United States blazoned forth the news that I had crossed the border, surrendered and was on my way to Chicago to stand re-trial. Consequently all along the route, wherever my train stopped, railway stations large and small were jammed with crowds waiting to see me. They swooped upon my train almost threatening forcible entry into my coach in an effort to see me, if I failed to make an appearance. It was a memorable journey. All the way I rejoiced in the realization that I was back on my native soil. That I probably would be compelled to serve a prison term, after all, was incidental. Of that I thought very little. That I was back in my own country was enough, and I was willing and capable of paying all the penalty that might be exacted from me for the privilege of regaining the home and friends that I so treasured.

It was originally intended that I should come to Chicago, but when it was learned that an unusual demonstration might take place on my arrival, plans were changed and arrangements were made to have me leave the train at Joliet. The demonstration which interrupted the program would not have been a hostile one. As it was, thousands of people gathered at the railway station where it was thought I was to leave the train. Many of these awaited me merely out of curiosity and were eager to see the ex-heavy-weight champion and the man who had caused such a stir in court and ring circles. Others however, composed of those of my own race and of white people were friends, intent on seeing that I had a fair deal and meaning to aid in preventing any undue persecution that might develop as a result of my return. It was not a mob as some newspapers hinted. The crowd was an orderly one and it was also a disappointed one when it was learned that I had been taken from the train at Joliet.

I was placed in prison at Joliet to await trial at Chicago. Newspaper writers, photographers and amusement promoters flocked about me. They invaded my prison quarters. The newspaper men were eager for interviews with me from which they constructed stories for the public that often were vastly contrary to the information I had given them. The promoters were anxious to sign me up for various stage and public appearances. Many of them apparently thought that I was soon to be freed of the charges against me, and some of them even went so far as to announce that they had made contracts for me to appear under their direction. These were mis-statements and were responsible in large measure for the court dealing with me more strictly than might have been the case. Judge Carpenter, in passing sentence upon me, later hinted that these announcements smacked of too much assurance that I had nothing to fear from the court. The newspapers printed many garbled stories concerning me, among them being those to the effect that I was not treated in the Joliet jail as a prisoner, but was permitted such privileges and freedom of conduct as to make the action of the prison officials illegal. These stories aroused bitter criticism and complaint, and as a result I was removed from the Joliet prison to Geneva. As a matter of fact, I was treated better in the latter prison than in Joliet. I was made a trusty at the outset and assigned duties that often took me outside the prison, where I remained at my own discretion. I also was made a turnkey, in which capacity I had charge of several prisoners, whose liberty in the jail increased or diminished according to my judgment. I remained in this jail for about three months or until October, 1920, when I was taken to Chicago for trial, the nature and result of which I have related in another chapter. The sentence imposed upon me, as I have said, I considered unjust, and the shadowing and persecution that followed had originally precipitated my flight.

Soon after the sentence, I was placed in charge of a United States Marshal, and accompanied by my friend, Jerry Brown, taken to Leavenworth to begin the prison term of a year and a day. The trip to the federal prison was made by way of Kansas City, Missouri, where there was a wait of several hours. During this period, on my promise to meet him at train time, the Marshal allowed me to make some hurried visits to friends in the city unaccompanied, and true to my promise to him, I joined him at the Union station, resuming the last leg of the trip that was to place me behind prison gates.

Prison officials were not surprised at my arrival, but I found that many surprises awaited me. Preparations had been made in advance for me, and after I had gone through the formality of "checking in," I was assigned to my quarters and supplied with the regulation prison garb and other equipment. My first surprise came when I was presented with the suit of blue denim which was to be my prison uniform. The man who had planned its dimensions must have used his imagination rather than a tape measure, and there must have been a liberal supply of material when the suit was constructed, for it was large enough for a tent and would have held me and several others like me. It was necessary to put through an emergency order for another suit before I could be properly arrayed.

Soon after my entrance, Warden Anderson and Deputy Warden Fletcher summoned me for an interview with them, in which they questioned me concerning my talents and the manner in which I wished to occupy my time inside the prison walls. From the outset both wardens were kind to me and I shall never cease to be grateful for their consideration and help. I was told by them that they wished me to keep up my physical condition, and to direct my efforts during the term I was to serve in a way that would benefit myself and the prison as well. Warden Anderson assured me that it was his wish to discharge me a better man physically and otherwise than I was when I entered the prison. In this purpose I believe he attained a signal success. By this I do not mean that the prison discipline improved me morally, but my stay in the prison, cutting me off as it did from the perplexities and strife of life, gave me time to take stock of my friends and my enemies. I came to the conclusion that one of my greatest errors was my flight to Europe, that I might avoid the disgrace and ordeal of prison. While to all intents and purposes, I had a delightful time in my travels and learned much concerning the world, I was, nevertheless, an unhappy and restless individual. During the years in which I was a fugitive nothing came into my life in the way of adequate compensation for the stings and grief I suffered over my separation from my friends and relatives, and particularly keen was the regret that I had not remained with my mother, or as close to her as I could. I was not given to melancholy contemplation of my situation, because there was much within the prison that stirred my interest and kept me alert.

After a day or two in the prison Warden Anderson introduced me to a man who, he said, was an old acquaintance of mine. At first I did not recognize him, but a word or two stirred pleasant recollections which echoed from one of the very important events of my life. The friend referred to was former Governor Dickerson of Nevada, who was the chief executive of that state when I fought Jeffries at Reno in 1910. Mr. Dickerson was serving in the capacity of prison superintendent, in which connection it proved later, I was to have much association with him. Dickerson, like the warden and his deputy, manifested much interest in me and proffered me his aid if ever I should need it. It was doubly pleasing to have his assurance of friendship, and to recall that we had formerly met at a time when I was facing a severe contest. On that occasion, too, he had extended me his friendship. My first meeting with Governor Dickerson came soon after my arrival in Reno, and while I was in training for the fight we met often. The governor, an ardent sportsman, was interested deeply in the training camps of both Jeffries and myself. He visited me frequently and discussed with keen interest the fight in which I was about to engage. He asked me if I thought I would win. I replied that I intended to do my best, and that I would win even though I broke an arm. He also asked me if I had any fear of Jeffries to which I answered with an emphatic "no." He questioned me also concerning rumors to the effect that they were "going to get me, even if it was necessary to use a bullet." I assured him that I was not frightened over these alleged threats, and that I placed no credence in them. He was not so sure however, and insisted on providing me with a guard of five state rangers. During the period of my training some of these rangers or all were constantly near me, and they with others were at the ring side on the day of the fight in order to forestall any attempt that might be made on my life. Governor Dickerson was determined that I should have a fair chance in that fight, and he left nothing undone that would provide it. Shortly before the fight, he told me, he had placed a bet on me. Later, I learned this bet amounted to several thousand dollars.

Throughout my prison term, the former Nevada governor was a staunch friend and adviser, and I was impressed through his interest in me, with the fact that one of the greatest things in the world is friendship. There is nothing which brings deeper satisfaction than the assurance of possessing loyal friends. They are rare and valuable, and there is nothing that should be more carefully guarded than these friends, particularly those whose confidence remains intact when circumstances place you in an unfavorable light and give room for criticism which seems unanswerable.

It did not take the prison authorities long to decide in what manner I should occupy myself in the prison. The post of physical director was soon created for me, and I was given charge of all athletic work. All prisoners wishing to engage in field or gymnasium activities were assigned to me. There virtually was none over me and there was no one to whom I was answerable in the performance of my duties in the prison excepting the executives. I had supervision of the baseball field, the prison track area, the gymnasium and all forms of athletics. I sought out those interested in boxing and gave them special training, and there were many snappy bouts staged between the more clever of the glove wielders in the prison. From this it will be gathered that whatever else I may have been denied as a prisoner, I was not compelled to give up the work which had been my chief concern in life.

In all, my imprisonment was in no wise as severe as I had anticipated. In many ways, I believe, I was the means of doing much good among the prisoners and for the prison. As a rule a man has no cause for congratulation over the fact that he has been compelled to forfeit his liberty, even for a short time. There is, at best, no attraction in prison life, and the thought that one is living under such discomforts and inconveniences as prison discipline imposes is not comforting. Yet I do not feel that the months I spent in Leavenworth were wasted.

My work as physical director kept me busy and interested. I had many duties and obligations, notwithstanding which, I gave considerable attention to the conduct of my personal and business affairs outside the prison. My business interests I did not neglect at any time, for I was looking ahead to the day when I would have paid the price, regained my freedom, and resumed my place in normal activities. Rhodes continued to act as my secretary and manager. He spent much time with me in my prison quarters, making many trips back and forth between Chicago and Leavenworth. In this manner I was enabled to keep in close touch with world affairs and such matters as pertained to my personal welfare. My wife, too, who made her home with my relatives during the time I was behind the walls, watched my business affairs closely and successfully. The combined efforts of Mrs. Johnson and Rhodes kept matters in satisfactory condition, so that when I was liberated I was ready to take up and carry on in such a manner that I was scarcely aware of any loss that might have been occasioned because of my enforced absence. Mrs. Johnson also was a frequent visitor at the prison, and her presence and continued confidence in me was a source of strength and inspiration that contributed greatly to my patience, and maintained my hope.

Without wishing to boast, I am tempted to record that my conduct in prison won for me a shortening of the original term. My record for good behavior was such that I was discharged after serving eight months of the year and a day for which I was sentenced. On the day I left the prison, many close friends came to meet me at the gates, but further than that there was a sort of general celebration, the extent and nature of which surprised and disconcerted me. There were four bands taking part in the demonstration. Hundreds of people whose cars were parked all over the prison grounds awaited my appearance and swarmed about me, once I had re-entered the outer world. They cheered and congratulated me, and if I had ever felt that my life had been a failure or that there was nothing further for me to accomplish, I changed my opinion at that moment and found myself rejoicing, eager and confident.

One outstanding event of the period of my imprisonment took place on Thanksgiving day when I appeared in the ring especially built within the prison walls, and fought two men, over each of whom I was the victor. It was not the fight particularly which impressed itself upon me, for fights have been so numerous in my life that they, with some exceptions, were only incidents. The Thanksgiving day event, however, was a gala one for the prison, and I am told that nothing ever took place in the prison's history which was characterized by more ceremony or excitement. My opponents in the ring were Topeka Jack Johnson, a former sparring partner and George Owen, a 227 pound boxer who had been brought from Chicago for the occasion. Attending the fight were more than a thousand inmates of the prison and several notable persons of Kansas and Missouri, many of them state officials. The fight took place in mid-afternoon, but guests and spectators began arriving before noon. An hour before the preliminaries began, the seating capacity was entirely exhausted and improvised seats, gathered from every corner of the prison, were hurriedly placed. The prison bands were out in force and played march tunes as the spectators took their seats. The bands also, blared forth when I took my place in the ring. As I looked about me I saw that several special guests were present and that among them were well known sportsmen and newspaper writers. According to the latter my skill and form was equal to any former occasion on which I attempted to entertain the public. I knocked Owen out in six rounds. The go between Topeka Jack Johnson and myself was more of an exhibition affair, and it was said of us by those who were competent judges, that our bout was a fast and classy one. Certain it is, the old prison had an awakening that day unlike any that had gone before it.

There were no particularly unpleasant incidents during my imprisonment, at least none in which I was concerned. I found little cause for complaint and outside the fact that I chafed under the ordeal of restriction from the outside world, my life was pleasant and comfortable. Only once was my temper aroused and that was occasioned when a man, actuated by the desire to make a dollar, substituted a roasted cat for an opossum which I had asked him to obtain for me. I had, with the permission of prison authorities, arranged with a hunter to get the opossum. He was unable to find one, and rather than lose the dollar which I had promised him, killed and dressed a cat, being careful to remove all parts of the animal which would reveal its identity. The cook who was delegated to prepare the animal for me was unfamiliar with opossum meat and unwittingly served the feline flesh with approved opossum trimmings. I had invited two or three friends to dine with me, but before we had partaken of the delicacy which we had anticipated with watering mouths, the deception was discovered. It was a disappointing dinner affair, but my disappointment was not as severe as my anger. Had I been able to lay my hands on the hunter at that moment, I fear that I would have treated him rather roughly. When my anger had subsided I tried to view the matter as a joke, but I failed in this. I was too big to deal with the offender as I wished, but I made arrangements with a smaller man to deal with the hunter, and according to reports which reached me, he paid dearly for the dollar which he had pocketed.

I left the prison in June, 1920. On the evening of the day on which I was liberated, I found myself in a role quite different from any which I had previously carried. I had been a boxer, a bull-fighter, a wrestler, an advertising man, an actor, a promoter, a clerk, a mechanic and a musician—now I was to be a lecturer. The lecture took place in one of the large halls of Leavenworth, and was under the direction of one of the prison chaplains. I had no particular subject but wandered around in a rather extensive field having for my topics religion, squareness, courage and successful living. As large as the hall was, it was unable to hold all who sought admittance, a large crowd having been turned away. In the audience were both white people and those of my own race. Just how well I acquitted myself, I will not attempt to say. However, I was conscious of the fact that I held the interest of my auditors, and I was assured that my talk was a good one.

I found material for my address in the information I had gained and the observations I had made while in prison for I was much given to studying the men and conditions about me. I made the acquaintance of many types of men in the prison. There were criminals of all degrees and they were paying penalties for offenses of many kinds. Some were hardened, bitter and dangerous; others were gentle, patient and without the slightest evidence of baseness. Some had served many terms, and some were serving their first term with the prospect, judging from their conduct within the walls, of serving additional terms. I learned that men who are criminals by instinct or inclination, always will be criminals, and that prison discipline will never deter them from being criminals. I also learned that men who are criminals by accident or from force of circumstances, and in whom there are no natural tendencies toward crime become criminals, as a result of imprisonment and their contact with other criminals.

Long and repeated prison terms have no effect in turning the evil doer from his path. His confinement only gives him opportunity to nurse his bitterness and to plan new exploits when he is out of prison. He is actuated by a desire to repeat his offenses believing that he can escape future capture or punishment by profiting by whatever mistakes he might have made in covering up former crimes. He has the constant desire to outwit the police and courts, whom he considers his enemies bent on accomplishing his destruction. His association with other criminals implants new ideas within him and he is always on the alert to obtain information from those of his kind, which he believes will prove helpful to him in his activities as a law-breaker. For men who have chanced into prison through a temporary lapse, because of a mistake, or due to unfortunate circumstances, and in whom there are no natural germs of criminality, long prison terms serve only to arouse bitterness. They have time to contemplate their misfortune, and most men of this class feel that they have been so thoroughly disgraced that they never again can appear in decent society. They are unwittingly influenced by the hardened criminals, and when they are once liberated, they have been saturated with ideas that will ultimately prove their undoing, and defeat the purpose of punishment or discipline as established by law. For a man who has committed an offense, the penalty for which is prison, if it is his first, and is committed without intent of criminal practice, a very short prison term will prove as efficacious, and will do more to protect society and himself than a long and arduous sentence. I believe there should be a schedule of prison terms devised which will enable courts to impose sentences according to individual temperaments, and the past records of accused persons.

After my discharge from prison, several business propositions demanded my attention. I had been considering numerous plans prior to my release but had not decided on a definite course. I was offered several theatrical engagements. Some were rather attractive, but I was not eager to leap into the limelight such as would mark my return to the stage. However, after my lecture in Leavenworth, I filled a short engagement at Kansas City and then went to Chicago with my wife. I received a splendid welcome on my return but did not remain long. I visited with my relatives and friends a few days and went to New York.

Upon my arrival there, I was accorded the greatest ovation by the people of my race and the public in general that I had ever received. A grand ball sponsored by Barron Wilkins and Dick Ellis, well known sporting men of the city, was staged for me and thousands of people were in attendance. My presence in the metropolis was for the purpose of lecturing in some of the churches, and I fulfilled several engagements discussing political, racial and other topics. At the conclusion of these lectures, I signed some vaudeville contracts covering a period of two months and calling for my appearance in New York City, Philadelphia and Pittsburgh. When these were finished, I returned to New York and organized an all-star vaudeville show, in which all the performers excepting myself were white. In this show

I did some comedy and exhibition boxing and did other stage work in conjunction with the other members of the troop. Our show was on the road twenty-five weeks, during which time we visited Chicago and most of the larger middle western cities. The venture was a prosperous one, but I was urged by an inclination to retire from the stage, and in casting about for another line of business, selected one which was not only entirely new to me, but which differed vastly from my previous experiences and associations. My new venture was in the brokerage field. I opened offices at 49th and Broadway, and engaged in selling stocks and bonds. I was more successful in this undertaking than might have been expected, inasmuch as it was a business the nature of which was entirely foreign to either my experience or temperament. In spite of these limitations, my efforts were not without success. I established no unusual records and the profits of the enterprise were not so large that I could not handle them. But when I gave up the business after several months, I did so with a clear conscience and with no liabilities hanging over me, which was more than could be said of many others whose capital and experience was much greater than what I had invested.

After my release from prison, I made no serious efforts to arrange any boxing matches, though I was by no means doubtful of my ability, and I lost no opportunity to emphasize my willingness to meet any man in the world. I had had my triumphs and the bitterness which accompanied them in my case. Yet, had circumstances been so arranged as to make a meeting between Jack Dempsey and myself possible, I would eagerly have gone into the ring with him. At no time in my life had

I neglected my physical health, nor had I failed to maintain a regular schedule of physical culture and gymnastic work. I had reached an age when popular belief assumes that a man must retire from ring or athletic exploits, and this belief was against me. But, as I said, I had not entertained serious intentions of engaging in spectacular ring contests, though I knew myself capable of doing so. My efforts to engage in other lines of business were only half-hearted, because I could not bring myself to ignore boxing, nor cease to believe that I had the old-time speed and punch.

Early in 1924, though I had reached the age of 46, the Montreal boxing commission after a thorough examination of me, declared that I was fit for ring work and issued me a boxing license. Armed with this, I signed for a ten-round go with Homer Smith of Kalamazoo, Michigan, who had whipped several heavyweights and who was acquiring a reputation for a "pile driving punch." The fight took place before the Montreal Athletic Club and was attended by one of the largest crowds ever patronizing a fight in that city. It was a sorry failure, however, and added nothing to my prestige, because Smith would not fight. Throughout the ten rounds he was at my mercy, and it would have been inhuman for me to take advantage of his weak efforts. I coaxed him to fight and the crowd jeered, but it was no use. After I had knocked him down sixteen times the contest ended quietly with the decision unanimously in my favor. One thing, however, was established by the fight and the training I did preceding it. Newspaper writers conceded that I had disproved the fact that age is a disqualifying element before youth in athletic contests. Sport writers who were prejudiced against me, grudgingly conceded that despite my long years in the ring, I had my old time skill and still wielded my famous punches with as much vigor as ever. That they were correct in their surmises, I confirmed more than two years later or on May 3, 1926, when at the age of 48 I won the decision over Pat Lester, a 24-year-old fighter, much larger than myself, whom I fought with comparative ease through fifteen rounds. The fight took place in Nogales, Sonora, Mexico, and I shall have something more to say concerning it in another chapter.

Following the Homer Smith bout, I appeared in several exhibition matches in Montreal and other parts of Canada, but there were no fighters in that country of sufficient experience or skill to make a satisfactory match with me, and I was confronted again with the lack of contestants and a consequent necessity of turning my attention to other lines of endeavor. This new enterprise took me for the second time into the advertising field in which capacity I was employed by a Canadian Brewery Company.

If I had begun to think that my troubles and griefs were over I was due for a rude awakening, for while it seemed that I was steering into quieter and smoother waters than had ever before characterized my life, some new domestic griefs reared themselves in my path. Echoes of the old wrath which my mother-in-law, Mrs. Cameron, nursed against me, came out of the past and Lucille, after twelve years of a marriage that had been a happy and successful one, obtained a divorce in New York City. Another romance had come to a sudden end. Our love, after many years of trials and tests through which it endured, was destined to fade. She had been in my life longer than any other woman and had enjoyed with me some of my greatest triumphs and suffered with me some of my greatest hardships and sorrows. She was always loyal and steadfast and she possessed a pluck and courage that enabled her to stand up bravely under many arduous experiences.

# CHAPTER VIII

## Adventures on Highways and Byways

THERE are few countries in which I have not traveled. I have not only loitered along the beaten paths of the old and new worlds, but I have gone into many strange and out-of-the-way corners of the globe and mingled with strange and little known people. I have rubbed elbows with the aristocrats of the European capitals; mingled with the frivolous in the noted cafés and restaurants of the continent; I have disported on the French and Italian Rivieras; I have been a guest in some of the finest homes of Mayfair, in London, where the élite and semi-royalty gathered in staid and dignified receptions. I have frequented exclusive clubs in St. James Street, London, and attended gatherings of notables in Paris. In Moscow my associates were Russian field marshals and aids of Czar Nicholas; in Budapest, Bucharest and Vienna my haunts were among some of the most wonderful clubs and restaurants in the world, where I met artists, scientists, writers and idle rich; in Australia I was the guest of notable men of that country. Having thus often found myself in the most exclusive circles of men the world over, I have on the other hand leaped to the other extreme and lived side by side with the aborigines and savages of the South Seas, of the Fiji Islands, and the Hinterland in Australia; the provincials of French and English possessions; the semi-savages—the Yaqui of Mexico; ruffians and adventurers of South America and the West Indies. I have been on the seas with smuggling crews and been a fellow-passenger of Chinese coolies who were being smuggled across the border from Mexico into the United

States. I have had opportunities to observe denizens of the underworld in nearly every country of the world; I have witnessed scenes among them that have no parallel even in the most imaginative fiction of melodramatic writers.

It is not my purpose to enter into a routine account of my travels, nor to attempt any description of the geography, commerce, races or customs of the lands and peoples I have learned to know. That has been done too many times by others more accomplished than I in the art of the narrative, and there is nothing I could add that would be new or interesting. Since this, however, is a personal account of my experiences I shall dwell only on certain outstanding happenings and situations in which I was concerned, not that they depict me in any particularly favorable light, or brand me as a globetrotter, but because I believe they will entertain and amuse my readers.

There is much I could write about the great World War, because I was in close contact with events immediately preceding that catastrophe and situations which came to pass in the first few months of the conflict. But of this, I am going to say little more, for that subject has been discussed and written about so voluminously that there is not much left for me to say. Elsewhere in this volume I have related my experiences in Moscow, where my party and I were arranging a series of public engagements when the war suddenly was precipitated upon the world. I have told of my close contact with military leaders and confidential advisors of the czar, of our sudden leave of that country and the adventurous journey through the war-frightened countries back to Paris and London.

When we were back in the French capital from the Russian center of war preparations, we found the country in chaos. Everything was being turned to war and its demands. Private citizens were being deprived of their automobiles and everything that could be used to resist the threatened invasion of the Germans. Being an American citizen, I was permitted to retain my automobiles, and as a result, we were able to travel extensively over France, and to see at close range the intense process of preparing for war.

Not long after our return from Moscow, we determined to go to London, and, loading our two cars with what possessions we had left, we started for the French coast from where we were to embark for England. For several days we had been within sound of the terrible gun-fire on the battle front, and not infrequently we had been directly under fire, having more than once traveled within a short distance of the battle lines. When we reached Boulogne, we realized the vast proportions the war was assuming because we encountered the first British troops to arrive on French soil. They were disembarking upon our arrival, and the sight was one that will never be forgotten. Speed was one of the factors entering into the war at that time, for the Germans were getting dangerously near. Regiment after regiment of English soldiers which had been hurriedly mobilized were leaving the boats with their equipment, and were immediately being marched away to the front.

It was at Boulogne that we had an experience that I can number among the many which nearly cost our lives. Cavalry and artillery horses belonging to the English troops were being unloaded from the boats and herded into every possible vacant space. It was pitch dark, lights having been strictly prohibited because of the dangers of air raids. It was almost impossible for the troops to pick their way from their transports, and the handling of the thousands of horses under these circumstances was a difficult task. There was a high pitch of tenseness on the part of both men and beasts. Everywhere there was an anxiety and an awe that was overwhelming. Suddenly, we became aware of a terrific disturbance. There was a rush of horses and human beings in the dark; thousands of hoofs were heard pounding in every direction, and at the same time there arose the shouts of alarm and fright of thousands of people.

The next minute there was added to this din the shrieks and groans of those who were in pain. We were in our cars, and about us came swirling masses of horses. More than 4,000 artillery and cavalry horses had got beyond control of the troops and were in mad stampede. The brutes, frightened as a result of their rough trip across the channel during which they had been unmercifully tossed back and forth across the stock decks of the boats, were in a highly excited state when it came to unloading them. We had noted previously that they were rearing, kicking, plunging and tearing about, but now with a suddenness that bewildered their herders, the thousands of troops, and a large proportion of the population of that French section, they had broken away and were roaring and milling about in the dark, trampling everything before them. They raced snorting over a wide territory, plunging into the troops and groups of citizens, many of whose bodies were mangled under their hoofs. Many persons were killed and hundreds were injured in the mad rush. Though we were in the midst of all this chaos, we were uninjured, being fortunate enough to be protected by our cars, but there were times when we feared they would either leap into the cars or turn them over in the furious jam.

While we were waiting at Boulogne for the boat that was to take us to England, news came to us of a terrible slaying of French soldiers which had taken place near us. The conflict in which they died was one in which they had killed one another by the thousands, their own artillery having raked the infantry and other units with deadly results. This horrible event was due to a trick which the Germans had planned. They had arrayed several of their own troops in French uniforms, the purpose being to get within the French lines, upon which they would have turned and dealt an overwhelming defeat. The French, however, discovered the deception. They had become aware of the approach of the enemy in their own uniforms and had turned their guns upon them. In the confusion that followed, the movement of the struggling regiments brought several units of French soldiers within range of their own guns, and the defending troops believing that the soldiers surrounding them or attempting to surround them were Germans proceeded to pour death upon them.

In this trap, thousands of Frenchmen were slain and wounded. Many of the latter were brought into the Boulogne section, and hearing that one of the wounded was a friend, I obtained permission to search for him. I found him in one of the emergency hospitals. His name was Cerf, a well known Paris sportsman, who with Theodore Vianne, another Paris man, had first intended to promote my fight with Moran. My erstwhile sporting friend was mangled by bullets, and the lower half of his face had been entirely shot away. It seemed impossible that he could live, and yet he did, though the disfigurement he suffered was most awful to look upon. On my visit to Cerf, I found with regret that many of my former Paris friends and acquaintances were among the wounded who had survived the trap. How many of my former associates had been killed I do not know, but I imagine there were many.

On reaching London after this experience, I signed a contract to appear at the South London Theater in the Elephant and Castle district, and hardly had our show been under way when the theater became a favorite target for air raiders. One night shortly after the opening of the show, bombs began to drop all around the theater and my audience was in panic. They attempted to rush from the house, but I stopped them. Hurrying to the footlights, I begged them to be still a moment. I told them that rushing from the theater as they were about to do, would cause more deaths than the bombs.

"Stay inside," I told them. "It is safer in here than out in the open." They were quieted and resumed their seats, but the situation was a tense and unpleasant one. Fear gripped the audience, and although we tried to continue with the show in order to distract their attention from the bursting bombs which were falling all around us, it was more or less of a failure. Finally the raiders departed, and the audience was dismissed. When we ventured out, we found the streets full of wreckage. Thousands of windows had been shattered and many buildings had been demolished. I had a dinner engagement that night after the show with some Americans who were visiting in London, and, entering my car, I attempted to reach the scene of the appointment. I found it impossible to travel over the course necessary for me to take because of the great piles of glass and other debris in the streets which blocked my car. Everywhere we looked we saw windowless buildings.

Unable to reach the home of my friends, I turned the car toward my home in the Haverstock Hill section. But the trip was not to be made undisturbed, for suddenly there came roaring out of the black sky more bombs. The raiders had returned. Between blasts of bombs which were falling all around us, we could hear the whir and swish of the Zeppelin overhead. I speeded the car up in an effort to get outside its bombing radius, but was surprised to learn that no matter how fast I traveled or in what direction I turned, the bombs were close upon us. It was then I learned with considerable alarm that the Zeppelin was following us. My car was a white Benz, and must have loomed up conspicuously to the raiders, who found it a tempting target. They persisted in the chase until I reached home, and I scrambled under shelter with all the haste I could summon. It was a miracle that we were not blown to bits. How we escaped I do not know. When we were under shelter, the Zeppelin did not desist, but remained over that section of the city for a long time, dropping countless bombs. When we ventured out the following morning, we viewed a scene of desolation. Many homes and public buildings had been hit by bombs, and a railway station a few blocks from us was completely demolished. That night, many persons were killed in several parts of the city, many of them in the neighborhood in which my home was located. The horrors of that night remain indelibly impressed on my memory and I still have a few shudders when I recall them.

In my travels throughout the world, I have been

caught in the turmoil of several revolutions, in which warring elements were striving for control of governments, and in which blood-shed took place on a far greater scale than the American people realize because of the meager news-reports which they have concerning them. I have been in revolutions in Spain, Portugal, Brazil, Mexico and Cuba. In most of these clashes I have been recognized as a neutral because of my non-citizenship, and was not purposely molested nor deliberately subjected to danger, but notwithstanding this, I have had some hair-breadth escapes and frequently have come near being the repository for a bullet intended for some other person.

On one occasion, in Barcelona, Spain, when that district aspired to secede from the Spanish government and set up an independent state, I was caught in the fire between the rebels and the government troops. Bullets whizzed about me with a recklessness that made me decidedly uncomfortable, and I saw myself stretched out like a human sieve. There is no doubt but that I would have been had I not been accompanied at the time by Chicorita, a well known Spanish bull fighter, who, incidentally, in the early part of 1927 was a visitor in Chicago. Chicorita knew how to conduct himself under such emergencies as we had encountered, and when the bullets commenced to spin about us, he jerked a white handkerchief from his pocket and waved it aloft. With the handkerchief waving above our heads, signifying that we were neutral, or at least ready to surrender, we sprinted down the Barcelona street with a speed that would have broken all running records, if there had been an official scorekeeper to make a note of it.

During this particular revolution, I was accorded

every courtesy by the contending factions, and was afforded all possible protection for my home. I was the only resident in Barcelona who was permitted to draw his window curtains, all others being compelled to keep their shades up so that soldiers could look within the houses when they wished, and to prevent snipers from hiding behind curtains and picking their opponents off in the street by gun-fire. In other revolutions I was considerably inconvenienced at times and compelled to remain under cover, but never was I in such danger as when Chicorita and I sped to cover under the protection of the white handkerchief.

On another occasion, when my party and I were in Montevideo, Uruguay, a revolution broke out. Although it was being waged for political control, each of the contending sides had fixed their interest and attention upon the banks and cash depositories of the country. I had been taking part in several profitable boxing exhibitions, and had at this time accumulated a considerable bank account. Learning the precarious conditions of the Uruguayan banks, I made haste to withdraw all my money. I had about $20,000. I could find no place of safety for it, because there was no place beyond the reach of the revolutionists who were pillaging right and left. As a result of this situation, I carried my money about with me, wherever I went. I placed it in a bag and devoted my entire time and attention to guarding it. When I visited friends or took part in business engagements, I retained a firm grasp on that bag. It was near my finger tips when I sat down to eat in the restaurants. When I went to the theater, I held fast to it; when I slept, the last thing I did was to fasten my fingers firmly about it. Wherever Jack Johnson went in that disturbed country, that money bag was close at hand, and when he left the country its contents was intact.

During my stay in Barcelona, I signed a contract to produce a moving picture, or rather to play a leading role in the picture. A Spanish company made the picture, and mindful of the popularity of American films sought to imitate some of the thrillers which had found their way into Spain. The title of the picture was "False Nobility." It was planned to have numerous sensational and breath-taking scenes. I had to rehearse scenes in which I, as the hero, had many narrow escapes from death. Some of these events proved more realistic than was intended and there were several times when I was considerably in doubt as to whether I would live to appear in the final scenes.

In one scene in which I was supposed to have been beaten and cast by my enemies into a jungle to die, a boa constrictor came near putting an end to my earthly existence. The snake had been obtained by the producer purposely for the scene. It was a giant, twenty-eight feet long, and had been an object of much interest on the part of members of the cast and others permitted to see it when "off stage," and to all intents and purposes seemed rather tame and gentle. In the picture scene, the reptile was supposed to crawl from its jungle home and come upon me lying helpless in the jungle waste. The plot of the scenario called for me to suddenly awake to the grim danger threatening me and to have a fight with the snake for my life. When the constrictor was released from his cage, he was not in a particularly energetic mood and resented being compelled to move out. It was necessary to prod him considerably and to drive him into the synthetic jungle at just the right spot.

The result was that by the time it was necessary for our titanic struggle to take place, the snake was consumed with a grouch. He was in an ugly mood, and when he saw me in my lethargic position, he suddenly determined to vent his spite on me. As he emerged from the grass and under-brush, I was seized with chills and fever, and the cause was not the imaginary wounds which I was supposed to be suffering from. That snake did not look as kind and agreeable to me as he had when I had viewed him in his cage. I read a sinister intent in his flashing eyes as he fixed his gaze on me, and forgot all about the instructions I was to follow. I was supposed to battle the monster for my life. It was said that when coiled, he was nine feet high, but as I looked at him preparing to lunge at me, I made a hurried calculation to the effect that there must be some mistake in the figures, and that instead of being nine feet high, he was sixty-nine. I also calculated that my skill as a fighter had suffered a momentary lapse, but I found that I could sprint; I got away to a quick start, and Olympic track stars, had they seen me on that occasion, would have felt themselves disgraced. It was necessary for them to get another man for the part, and after serious contemplation I came to the conclusion that film making wasn't such an enjoyable occupation after all.

After a few days, when I had recovered from my meeting with the snake, I appeared on the picture lot again and was informed that I was to have a lion for a playing partner. I did not relish this idea, but I believed that a lion was much more companionable and susceptible to reasoning than a boa constrictor. My part with the lion was to take place in the jungle too. I had sought to put myself on friendly terms with him and whenever

I made a social call at his cage, he seemed to be possessed of a sweet and kindly disposition. I was assured that he was docile and would enter into his part of the picture-making with the utmost gentleness. But I had my doubts, and as it turned out these doubts were well founded. His cage was moved into the jungle scene and concealed by trees and shrubs. I, for the time being a nomadic wanderer, was supposed to be resting at the edge of the jungle, contemplating the beauties of nature or some such noble subject as that, when the lion was to spring upon me, and a fight was to take place that would bring movie spectators out of their seats gasping. I assumed my position as per instructions and awaited the leap of the lion, which was to be liberated from his cage behind the jungle growth by an attendant. But when he leaped, I was utterly unable to perform in a manner expected of moving picture heroes as they appear on the screen. When I saw that monster with his glaring eyes and wide open mouth flying through the air at me, I changed my mind about being a hero. A long wooden staff such as lion tamers use was to have been near at hand for me to seize in my tussle with the jungle king, but the property man had forgotten it, so I had nothing but my bare hands. But what I lacked in courage and muscle for that occasion, I made up in vocal demonstration.

"Get out," I yelled at the lion. I yelled some more and very loudly and excitedly too; in fact I yelled so loud that the lion took fright, changed his mind about devouring me and turned his tail, hiding himself in nearby woods, where he remained for several hours. As for me, I traveled in the opposite direction, and did not slacken my speed until assured that the lion was not on my trail. I told the director that I believed he would be able to play the part better than I. He thought the matter over a little while and decided that that particular part was not necessary for the success of the picture anyhow, and I heartily agreed with him, having been of that opinion from the beginning. To whatever extent that picture was finished, and however successful it proved, there is one thing certain—the waiting public did not see me vanquish the boa constrictor or choke the lion to death, as the director no doubt had intended.

I have always been an ardent motorist. I have driven a car nearly ever since the first models were available to the public. Never have I been without one, and during my ownership and operation of cars, a sample of nearly every good car manufactured has at one time or another been in my possession. I have owned nearly every make of American and many models of European cars. I have shipped my motors across the Atlantic and the Pacific as I engaged in traveling. With few exceptions, these cars were built for speed and the court records of several American cities and not a few European cities will attest to the fact that I took advantage of these qualities countless times. I never had an ambition to be a real speed demon, but I must confess to having a weakness for fast driving. I decided, however, that I was not cut out for a race driver, when on one occasion I entered a race with Barney Oldfield. The manner in which he out-drove and outstripped me, convinced me that I was not meant for that sport, but nevertheless I have been near death many times in auto clashes, and on five occasions my cars have turned completely over with me, each time demolishing the car, but always I escaped uninjured as did everyone riding with me, except once when my head was torn open and it was necessary for me to have twenty stitches in my scalp. Four of these turtle turning experiences were in 1925. One took place at Benton Harbor, Michigan, when I was driving Chicago-ward in a rain-storm, my speedometer indicating a speed of sixty miles an hour. In attempting to take a highway curve, my car refused to turn. Instead it plunged straight ahead. The front wheels caught and wedged in a culvert, and remained there, but the rest of the machine with myself and a wolf dog in it, was hurled forty feet. The car was splintered but I did not get a scratch. The wolf dog squirmed out of the wreckage some way, and I found him later several miles from the scene.

At another time my car turned over near Elgin, Illinois, three men riding with me were unhurt, but I suffered the injury in this accident which necessitated the several stitches I mentioned previously. When I was thrown some distance away from the wreck, I lighted near a small pile of pebbles, and when my companions came to my aid, one of them exclaimed:

"My God! His brains are running out."

This exclamation aroused me from my daze, and I felt my head to make sure that I was alive. I was hurried a short distance down the road to a doctor. When we arrived, he said he could not attend me because a man was dying in an accident near-by.

"I'm the accident," I replied. "They brought it to you."

The car was smashed to smithereens, as another car was near Cleveland when it turned over on the highway, when I took to the ditch to escape a collision. In this smash my passengers and I were uninjured.

# JACK JOHNSON

In 1924, while driving between Bridgeport and New Haven, Connecticut, my big touring car, traveling at top-steed, leaped from the highway and turned over several times. There was none injured at this time. In France in 1914 when I was on my way from Paris to Boulogne driving an Austin car at seventy-five miles an hour it left the road, went over a bank and plunged fifty feet. Neither myself, Mrs. Johnson nor Rhodes, who were with me at the time, were hurt, but there was **not** enough left of the car to tell what it had ever been.*

* After his release from Leavenworth, the only encounters Johnson had with the law involved speeding violations.

# CHAPTER IX

## CHASING THE CHAMPION

I CHASED Burns around the world in order to get him into the ring with me. It was a two-year job. When I finally faced him in Sydney, New South Wales, December 26, 1908, and won the championship, the occasion was a notable one in the history of the prize ring. It was unlike any other event in the boxing world, because it marked the first time that a man of my race had ever won the title. It was the first championship contest ever waged off American soil, and for the first time in ring annals, the promoter of the fight and the manager of one of the contestants served also as referee. My suggestion that Hugh McIntosh serve in the latter capacity was one of the last of countless concessions that I had made in my effort to get at Burns, who had side-stepped me for months, and who had imposed conditions, some of which were almost impossible, and none of which a man less eager than I, would have considered for a moment. I trailed Burns from New York to London, from London to Paris and back, and from London to Australia. Always he made excuses or whenever he did show a willingness to meet me, it was under terms which denied me any possible advantage, and virtually removed every inducement excepting the possibility of gaining the title. I was the object of much ridicule on the part of Burns and his friends and he had openly insulted me so many times by uttering unprintable remarks and by calling me "yellow," that, had I met him personally, he would have fared worse than he did in the ring at Sydney. But he was careful to avoid a personal meeting and hurled his insults at long range. For many months prior to the fight, there had been much bitterness between us. As the fight approached the tension increased, and a day or two before the ring meeting, came near assuming a rough and tumble clash, when he attempted to hit me with a chair.

My intensive chase after Burns began when I left San Francisco early in 1907, and went to New York, where Burns then was. I sought to arrange a meeting with him for the purpose of discussing a match, but he declined to meet me and soon afterward left for England. In the meantime, I engaged Sam Fitzpatrick as my manager, and we launched our campaign to go after the world title. Hattie McLay had joined me, and financed by her father, she, Fitzpatrick and I took up Burns' trail and followed him to London. He deftly escaped meeting me, but indulged in a lot of ill flavored remarks and threats concerning me. Soon after my arrival in London, I made several music hall engagements, which kept me so busy that I had little opportunity for training or keeping myself in shape.

Fitzpatrick was busy in planning bouts for me, and despite the unfavorable fighting condition I was in, made a match with Ben Taylor, who was then England's most promising heavy-weight, having defeated every possible contender. This match was based upon the craziest terms under which I ever fought, and in view of the important prospects at stake, I thought Fitzpatrick had suddenly lost his senses. Taylor was in fighting trim and was much heavier than I. I was in poor shape, yet Fitzpatrick had consented to terms which provided that to win, I must knock Taylor out in ten rounds; that the rounds were to go only two minutes each; and that we should use six-ounce gloves. Had I lost this fight, and there was a chance that I might, it would have meant a sudden end to my theatrical engagements, for I would have ceased to be an attraction. Furthermore it would have placed me in a class which would have prevented serious consideration of me as a contender for the title.

There was nothing for me to do but abide by Fitzpatrick's silly arrangements and I entered the ring with Taylor with my chance at the championship at stake. Fortunately, I was able to comply with the terms and knocked Taylor out in the ten rounds. Hardly had I finished this fight, when Fitz had another ready for me. It was Fred Drummond, whom I beat in a fairly fast go at Plymouth. The results of these fights were to raise me considerably in the esteem of the British public, which began to sit up and take more notice of me. The press and boxing authorities, if they ever had favored Burns, now became more friendly toward me, and recognized my claim on the privilege of meeting Burns, and backed me in those claims, taking occasion to direct much severe criticism upon the title holder.

I filled a few more theatrical engagements in London and Paris, while Burns left for Australia. I did not linger long in England, for my quarry having flitted, it was necessary for me to resume the pursuit. Accordingly, my party and I also set sail for Australia, where I eventually cornered Burns and arranged for our fight. It was my second visit to the Antipodes, and there were many friends to greet me. On my first visit, I had polished off Felix and Lang, two Australian fighting boys who were well thought of. This had won for me the respect of boxing enthusiasts, but there were not many who believed I had a chance with Burns, who was a prime favorite, because on two occasions he had knocked out Bill Squires, another Australian, who at one time had been a seven-days' wonder to the kangaroos. Because of his two defeats of Squires, Burns was considered unbeatable and was the prime betting favorite, the average odds against me being two to one.

In addition to Burns' popularity, and the belief that I could not defeat him, the rumor became prevalent that there was some crooked work abroad; that it was framed that I should lose, and that I was not to have a fair chance in the ring. These rumors helped sustain the betting odds, and friends and others who really believed I could whip Burns, bet their money on my opponent in the belief that the decision would go against me, despite whatever showing I made. I felt too, that there was something astir and knew that I should have to watch my step in the selection of the referee. This was no pleasant combination of circumstances under which to contest for the championship in a strange country, but I was determined that nothing would prevent me from going through, because I already had sacrificed most of the usual rights and privileges accorded a challenger, and had agreed to accept a trivial sum of money—$5,000 whether I won or lost, while Burns was to get $35,000 win or lose.

My, but I did train for that fight! My training camp was at Botany bay, and in my camp were Duke Mullins, chief adviser and second; Bobby Bryant, Leo O'Donnell, Rudolph Unholz, the Walker brothers, Jack and George, and other boxers, all of whom served me well as sparring partners, seconds and general aids. My condition was superb. I do not recall another pre-fight period in my life when I felt better or was more fit to enter the ring. My lungs were in especially fine condition, and no matter how strenuously I exerted myself it seemed that I never got winded. Although we were engaged in the serious business of preparing to fight the world champion, we had a gay time at that camp, and indulged in strange and at times rather frivolous amusements. We performed stunts that amazed the Australians and caused them to shake their heads as if they doubted our sanity.

In two of these stunts, I was the sole performer, and the manner in which I performed indicated the excellent condition of my breathing equipment. Half in jest, I had wagered with some of my friends that I could out-run a kangaroo. The wager was taken and it was up to me to back my assertion. Accordingly, we stirred up a kangaroo and the chase began. These animals, it is generally known, are able to cover distance with ease and the one with which I raced was no exception. How far I chased him, I do not know. Both of us were developing high speed, and each was determined to endure, but the poor kangaroo finally gave up and toppled over dead. He had completely exhausted all his strength and vitality. As for me, I was little the worse for the chase.

On another occasion, a greased razor-back pig was turned loose for me to catch. He was a long, tall and lanky member of his species, built like a race horse. Furthermore, he was undomesticated and valued his liberty exceedingly high. He had no wish to be coddled and manifested a rather vicious nature. Once turned loose, he endeavored to put as much space as possible between himself and mankind. But as speedy as he was, he was unable to out-run me. After a pursuit that included many turns, twists and other maneuvers, I grasped his oily body, and despite his struggles subdued him.

Imitating hounds in speed and cunning, Duke Mullins, Bobby Bryant and myself ran a jack-rabbit to death. These rodents are considered about the last word in animal speed and are used in Australia in hound chases. Our race with the rabbit took place on a half-mile dog racing track within an enclosure. The rabbit was turned loose with the three of us in pursuit. Our victim resorted to all his clever tricks in eluding his enemies, and traveled so fast at times that he looked like a streak, but he was not clever nor fast enough to escape us, although he ran until he fell exhausted.

These are not imaginary tales but are actual occurrences and were reported in the Sydney newspapers. These and other events at my camp were a source of much discussion among Sydney folk and because of the unusual things which we did in the course of enjoying ourselves, attracted many people daily to our camp, wondering what we would do next. They got a lot of entertainment out of it and my friends and acquaintances increased in number. Most of my training was done in the early morning. I did lots of road work but comparatively little boxing, giving my attention largely to ball and bag punching. This method of training also caused the Australians to marvel. They were not accustomed to such procedure. They were certain that I was not training properly and that I was most neglectful. They were convinced that I could not possibly be in shape for the fight, and this belief having gained circulation, also

On the Mexican–U.S. border, Johnson shakes hands with a California sheriff in 1920. With one step on American soil, Johnson would be under arrest for bail jumping in Chicago eight years earlier, on the Mann Act violation.

Johnson trains in Mexico for his 1920 fight with Bob Wilson by pitting his strength against two horses.

Johnson, 42, shows the same strength that knocked out Jim Jeffries in 1910, ten years earlier. He defeated Wilson in three rounds.

Johnson gets a ticket for speeding. Johnson died in a car accident in Raleigh, North Carolina, June 16, 1946.

Johnson and his manager, George Little, rode in automobiles when bicycles were still a common means of transportation.

Jack Johnson trains in Chicago, 1923.

Johnson and a group of friends and fighters, 1929. Ed Sullivan is third from left.

Johnson plays cards in Paris with his trainer, Bob Armstrong, seated on far right.

Johnson shakes hands with Cyclone Cooper, his sparring partner.

Johnson and his fourth wife, Irene, breakfast in Paris, 1933.

Johnson in Paris, 1933.

Irene shared her husband's interest in travel. Johnson wrote that his love for Irene paralleled no other love in his life.

During a New York interview in 1936, Johnson displays the smile that Jack London described as "golden" in 1910.

Johnson, 66, and Jess Willard, 60, meet again 30 years after the match in Havana. Willard died at the age of 83 on December 15, 1968.

Jack Johnson in retirement, 1945.

In 1936, Johnson made his operatic debut in "Aida".

The stage was not strange to the veteran music hall performer, Jack Johnson.

Jack Johnson, at 53, was still fighting exhibition bouts and proved to be in good condition.

Johnson at the 1934 Baer-Carnera fight in Madison Square Garden Bowl, Long Island, watches from the other side of the ropes.

Jack Johnson, the champ, 1909.

added to the conviction that Burns would have the best of me.

I never was sure of getting Burns into the ring until I faced him inside of the rope. After the fight agreement was signed and our training camps were established, Burns continued his old tactics of sidestepping and making excuses. He was not satisfied with the terms of the contract, even after he signed them. He had many complaints to make, and persisted in opposing various details of arrangements for the fight. I expected him to call the fight off any day. I myself remained silent and either ignored his objections or consented to measures that would remove them, so eager was I to insure his presence in the ring at the appointed time. I do not exaggerate when I say it was almost necessary to drag him into the ring, but once in the ring he was a game and determined fighter and he took the punishment I gave him gamely and tried hard to defend his title.

The selection of referee was one of the most difficult tasks in connection with the fight and sometimes assumed such proportions as to threaten interruption of the fight. It was the subject of much bitter controversy and afforded Burns much opportunity for stalling. There were referees whom Burns would have accepted, but sensing the possibilities of trickery, or at least of an arrangement that would not be to my advantage, I, too, became more cautious for I knew that there were men in Australia who, especially when the welfare of a favorite was at stake, would make decisions according to instructions, if the inducement was sufficient. We had several meetings for the purpose of discussing the referee and most of these were heated affairs.

# JACK JOHNSON

One evening I went to the office of Promoter McIntosh to take up the troublesome subject. The meeting was by appointment and those attending were Burns and his manager, Fitzpatrick, and myself. Accompanying me was Phyllis Bain, the seven-year-old daughter of James Bain, manager of the National Amphitheatre. Accompanied by her parents, the little girl was a frequent visitor at my camp. They were my dinner guests most every evening. Phyllis was quite fond of me and I of her. She insisted on going with me whenever I went to the city, on a drive or elsewhere. It was a rather unusual meeting for a child to attend. As our discussion progressed Burns became very angry.

"You used to be a good fighter," Burns said to me, "but you are all shot now; you might as well take your medicine."

I only smiled at this and other insults which he uttered, but when he began to use profanity and become obscene I ceased to smile and warned him to stop.

"Burns," I said, "the newspapers are describing you as a gentleman, so be careful what you say. If you swear any more before this child, I shall give you a lacing right here."

This angered him beyond endurance, and springing to his feet he made a gesture as though he would pull a gun, and I moved toward him. As I advanced, Burns grabbed a chair which was snatched from him by McIntosh. He then seized an inkwell which was standing on McIntosh's desk, but before he could hurl it, McIntosh grabbed his arm and attempted to hold him.

"Let him loose," I said to McIntosh. "He's tame and harmless." Then, turning to Burns, I said: "I'll remember this when I get you into the ring."

We came to no agreement that day. I returned to my training wondering what the outcome would be. In the following few days, Burns three times threatened to declare the fight off unless he could select a referee. As the day of the fight approached, they sent for me three times to go and discuss the referee, but I declined. I had decided that nothing was to be put over on me and had been working out a proposition which I proposed to spring at the proper time. Two days before the fight when all parties to the contract, the newspapers and the public were in suspense as to who would be the referee, or whether or not the fight would take place, I took Fitzpatrick with me and went to talk over the problem with McIntosh and Burns. I had been battling for time and still was, my intention being to delay the selection of the referee until the last possible moment. On the occasion of this, our last meeting I permitted the conversation to go on for several hours. I felt that Burns was seeking to call the fight off, but I did not intend that such a disappointment should ensue.

I knew that I could whip Burns in a fight staged on merit, regardless of whom he might pick as referee, and if I had been convinced that there would be fair play in the contest, I would never have bickered. I knew that Burns and McIntosh were the closest of friends and that each had the fullest confidence in the other. I knew that McIntosh, as promoter of the fight, would not dare give an unjust decision such as might be given by an outsider, and so after the futile discussion had gone on for some time, I sprang my proposal which was a surprise bomb to those present. I turned to Burns, who was sitting across from me, and said:

"Before going any further with this match, I want to know if you and McIntosh are good friends."

"We are friends, the best of friends," replied Burns.

Turning to McIntosh, I inquired: "How about it; are you and Burns good friends; do you have confidence in each other?"

"We are great friends; there are none better," he answered.

All this time, Fitzpatrick stood by without uttering a suggestion or comment. I addressed McIntosh again, saying,

"If you and Burns are such good friends, then you must referee this fight."

Fitzpatrick gasped in astonishment and began to frame a protest, but I interrupted him.

"I am fighting this fight and am going to have some part in naming the referee.

"Is it all right with you, Burns?" I asked.

He replied that it was. When I addressed the same query to McIntosh, he hesitated declaring that he had never had experience as a referee, and expressing his doubt as to whether or not he could qualify. I insisted that he should, and before we left the room, he had consented.

The next day it was given out to the newspapers that McIntosh was to referee the fight. At first, neither the papers nor the public believed the statement was true, and hundreds flocked to the training camps to ascertain for themselves whether or not it was so. The arrangement did not please the public and there was much sarcastic comment. When the announcement was confirmed, it had the effect of changing the betting odds.

Burns, who had been a 5 to 4 favorite during the last few days before the fight now became a 7 to 4 favorite, which clearly showed it was believed that the naming of McIntosh meant an advantage for Burns. Fight fans were never quite reconciled to the selection, and on the day of the fight when McIntosh entered the ring, he got a noticeably cool reception, compared with the cordial receptions given both Burns and myself. However, while my appearance created a ripple of applause, it was nothing to the ovation that was given Burns.

The fight was the greatest ever held in Australia. Twenty-five thousand spectators attended, thousands of them having formed in line twenty-four hours before the fight began in order to get seats. Although in the midst of strangers, many of whom were semi-hostile toward me, I was not in the least perturbed. I felt no doubt of the outcome, and had I not intended to give the crowd its money's worth, I could have finished Burns in the first few rounds. Then, too, I figured that Burns had something coming to him, and I proposed to extend his punishment over a considerable length of time. I certainly wished to give him his $35,000 worth. He found out after the first few blows that he was done for, but he kept coming, and I heartily commend him for his gameness. His blows had no strength and I do not recall that they as much as stung me. Certainly he never jarred me. I hit him at will, whenever I wished, but I never exerted my whole power on him.

In addition to his gameness Burns fought cleanly. Neither of us used any foul or tricky tactics, which made it easy for the inexperienced and somewhat nervous referee. Once or twice he tried to separate us in the clinches, but lacking the strength for such effort, he gave it up and left us to work out of them of our own accord.  Once in a clinch, he grabbed my wrist, which enabled Burns to land a blow on my face, but since it did not hurt me I made no complaint.  Burns on the contrary complained many times and frequently appealed to the referee.  My defense completely baffled Burns. I led brisk lefts and rights to his body and face, and administered an awful punishment to him.

I found my opponent easier than I had anticipated. I kept up a continual conversation with Burns and with those at the ring side, as I usually do in the ring.  Once with my hands at my side, I extended my chest and chin inviting Burns to hit me.  I made openings for him and called his attention to them.  "Find that yellow streak," I told him.  "You have had much to say about it; now uncover it."  At first, Burns tried to answer my sallies, but he soon desisted, his remarks being scarcely audible.

The intervals between rounds gave me a chance to scan the crowd and pick out unusual types of faces, or watch the changing expressions that flitted across the countenances of the spectators as they concentrated their attention on us.  I even had opportunity to examine the outlying landscape and the immediate structure around the ring.  As my gaze wandered out into the surrounding territory, I saw a colored man sitting on a fence watching the fight with open mouth and bulging eyes. My glance returned to him again and again.  He was one of the very few colored people present, and he became a sort of landmark for me.  I became more and more interested in him, and soon discovered that mentally, he was fighting harder than I was.  Whenever I unlimbered a blow, he, too, shot one into the air landing it on an imaginary antagonist at about the same spot where I landed on Burns. When I swayed to avert a blow from Burns, the fighter on the fence also swayed in the same direction and at a similar angle. When I ducked, he also ducked. But his battle came to an inglorious end when it was necessary for me to make an unusually low duck. He attempted to follow the movement and fell off the fence. This incident so amused me that I laughed heartily, and Burns and the spectators were at a loss to know what had so aroused my mirth. Jack London, the late story writer, and Mrs. London were ring-side spectators and I think it was at this time that London got the idea of the golden smile with which he often described me later and which was so frequently mentioned in after years.*

In the ninth and tenth rounds Burns was in a bad way. It would have been easy to have disposed of him, but so long as he invited more punishment I ladled it out to him as thick as he could stand it without going under. I eased up considerably in the last rounds, but in the fourteenth I decided to put an end to it. Just as I stepped out with this intention, I caught the eye of the police inspector. He had said nothing, but I felt that he was going to and I desisted from any further attack on Burns. I was not mistaken about the inspector's intention. "This has gone far enough," he said, and the fight came to an end. I had gained the title of champion of the world.

Friends and acquaintances, many of whom had lost money on Burns because of their fears that the fight would be unfair to me, swarmed upon me as I left the

---

* London later described the match in the *New York Herald* as a meet between "a pygmy and a colossus."

ring and poured forth their congratulations. Burns' friends helped him from the ring and hurried him to a doctor. I had suffered no discomforts in the bout and there was scarcely a scratch on me. After leaving my dressing room, I took a plunge in the surf, followed it up with a motor drive, and that evening entertained friends at dinner.

# CHAPTER X

## The Great Jeffries Bows

IT was virtually necessary for me to wage two ring battles before I established undisputed claim to the championship. My fight with Burns really gave me the title, for he was the recognized champion. When I acquired his laurels, the question suddenly arose as to whether or not Burns was the champion. It was stoutly declared by some that Jeffries was the champion, because he actually had not lost the title in the ring, merely having voluntarily relinquished it to Hart, who had been defeated by Burns. It was upon this basis that Burns claimed the championship, and it never was questioned until I established my claim. At any rate I was not permitted to rest secure in the title. I was constantly harassed and criticized. Those who conceded, but resented my rightful claim to the title, started a turmoil by hunting a "white hope" or one who would regain the title for the white race.

This hunt was a long and bitter one. All kinds of condemnation was heaped upon me—originating from no other cause than that I was not white. A large proportion of the public, or that part interested in boxing, at least, insisted that Jeffries still was the champion and that I must defeat him if I wished to retain the belt. I did not object to this proposal. I was willing to defend my claims against any man in the world. I lent my efforts and willingness to arrange a bout with Jeffries. It is interesting to note that Jeffries himself laid no

169

claim to the title. He had retired from the ring and wished to remain out of it. At first, he declined to fight and much pressure had to be brought upon him to induce him to consider a match. An insistent cry went up from the country—a demand that he fight. It was said he was the only "white hope" available and that he must meet me in order to keep the title in the possession of the white race. He had not fought for a long time, but he finally agreed to meet me, and it was arranged that we should fight July 4, 1910, at San Francisco.

This fight, too, was an historic one and stands out as one of the most unusual ring events in the world. A one-time champion—one of the greatest fighters in the history of pugilism, had been coaxed back to contend for the title in order to satisfy jealousy, hatred, and prejudice.

I deeply regretted this phase of the affair, but I was determined that I would defend my title and demonstrate that I was worthy of it. I knew that I could whip Jeffries. I was so willing to meet him, that I made many concessions, just as I had in the Burns fight, but being the title holder I did reserve the right to dictate some of the financial terms, as a result of which I was able to obtain a modest fortune which was really the most substantial returns I had ever received from my ring ventures. The fight was promoted and managed by Tex Rickard, and both he and I had our troubles with the affair. Throughout the whole business there were many difficulties and disappointments. It seemed that fate was working overtime to stop the fight or to make it a failure. Rickard at first wished to stage the fight in Salt Lake City, but Californians brought so much pressure upon him that he agreed to hold the mill in San Francisco. After he had obtained the license, built the arena and sold $300,000 worth of tickets, and Jeffries and myself had established training quarters in the San Francisco district, Governor Gillette suddenly forbade the fight giving no explanation for his action. Rickard lost $50,000 by that move, but undismayed he set out to find another site, and negotiated for holding the contest at Reno, Nevada, to which place it was necessary for us move our training quarters. As the plans for the fight progressed, strained relations developed between George Little, my manager, and myself. He had carried on the negotiations for the fight in my behalf, but while I was training events came to such an issue between him and me, that we separated and from then on, until the day of the fight, he carried on a campaign against me, based upon misunderstanding and falsification, that in the end proved disastrous to him and all who had listened to him.

Jeffries was very bitter toward me and indulged in many hateful and venomous remarks concerning me. He condemned me in scathing terms. For a long time he declared that he had drawn the color line. He attacked Burns for fighting me, saying that he was money-mad and that he had sold his pride and the pride of the Caucasian race by fighting me. Jeffries' father, a minister, said he would disown his son if he appeared in the ring with me, forgetting that his son, Jack, had been in the ring with me in 1902 and that both Jim and his brother, Jack, had previously fought men of my race. During all this long period while discussion of our fight was carried on, the ex-champion was engaged in the theatrical business. He devoted much time to denying that he would meet me, or informing the public what he would do in the event he did meet me. This talk, which filled the sporting pages, was good advertising for him and made his show business profitable, and when the articles were finally signed by us, he proceeded to make as much capital out of it as possible and there was no doubt but that because of his forthcoming meeting with me the public paid more willingly and liberally to see him on the stage. I bore no bitterness toward Jeffries; I said very little in reply to his taunts and criticisms further than to reiterate my wish and willingness to fight him. As the fight neared, ugly rumors were afloat concerning the "fixing" of the fight, and frequently it was declared that I was going to "lie down to Jeff." To these I paid little attention, though I admit that many circumstances developed which made the outcome seem doubtful to me.

My break with Little, my manager, coming as it did during the training period, caused the public to indulge in much speculation, and when he hinted that he had information to the effect that the fight was "fixed," letting it be known that this was the reason for splitting with me, the public was more than ready to believe it. Little circulated about freely at Reno, and became very friendly with members of the Jeffries camp. More than that, he bet heavily on Jeffries and that was the signal for many others, who originally intended to back me, to switch their money to Jeff. This also shot the betting odds upward. The fact is that the things that caused Little and me to separate were insignificant. They concerned the fight in no way and were not even based upon business relations. I liked Little, for he was a splendid fellow in many ways, but subject to erratic and hotheaded actions. When I learned that he was betting on

Jeff and hinting at crookedness on my part, I was not resentful as much as sorry for him and sent him word cautioning him not to be silly. "I am going to win this fight," I told him, "and if you do not want to lose your money you better not bet on Jeff." My warning had no effect upon him. He continued to put all the money he could raise on Jeff and urged his friends to do the same. The consequences to him and his friends, in a financial way, my readers can easily guess. Opposition to me was heightened and belief in the possibility of crookedness was increased when Sam Langford arrived on the scene and intimated that he had information to the effect that I was going to let Jeffries win. Perhaps Langford did think that Jeffries would win, but neither he nor any other had any except an imaginary reason to believe the fight was not on the square. Langford, however, disliked me, principally, I think, because I had defeated him, having given him a good beating at one time. At any rate, he bet on Jeff, and his friends and others followed his example. The results were disastrous for them, but preceding the fight, Langford's activities lent color to the rumors afloat concerning me.

Recently he was reported to have said in an interview for a magazine article that he found me an easy opponent, in spite of the fact that I defeated him. I have no desire to exaggerate my ability as a boxer nor to minimize the capacities of my opponents. Langford calls attention to the fact that he knocked me down to indicate that I did not have the best of him. If Mr. Langford really gave this interview, all that I can say is that, in the language of the prize ring, he is punch-crazy, for no such knocking down of me occurred. The fact is that I dropped him a few times during the encounter.

# JACK JOHNSON

The boxers and sport writers who witnessed the event, among whom I recall the names of Joe Walcott, Mike Twin Sullivan, and John Twin Sullivan, Stephen Mahoney, a noted Boston sport writer, and Alec McLean, fight promoter, will attest the truth of my remarks.

Now to go on with the story of the Johnson-Jeffries fight, because of the bitterness entertained by Jeff toward me, and the persistent hints concerning the fairness of the fight, and the importance with which it was fraught for me, the selection of the referee for the contest, like that in the Burns fight, was a difficult problem. The press and sporting authorities gave it much attention.* It was a matter of lengthy daily discussion by sport writers. Countless men were suggested for the task, but neither Jeffries, his manager nor myself could decide upon one that would be mutually satisfactory. We held many conferences over the proposition, and at times this phase was a troublesome one. It became the source of much speculation, and fight fans were considerably on edge because of the suspense that ensued. It was necessary for me to proceed with caution in the selection of a referee, because not only were the championship and a fortune at stake, but my reputation was involved. However, I brought this controversy to a satisfactory conclusion by suggesting that Rickard be the referee. He was acceptable to Jeff and his manager and consented to act in that capacity. Thus, for the second time in the history of prize-ring contests, the bout promoter was the referee, the other occasion being, as I have described, when I won the championship from Burns. Tex, I am pleased to say, proved entirely satisfactory and his decisions and his conduct of the fight throughout were such as to please all concerned. Despite the hatreds,

---

* Newspapers campaigned for a suitable referee. Irving Lewis of the *New York Telegraph* asked Sir Arthur Conan Doyle to referee the match. Doyle declined. He later wrote, "I was much inclined to accept this honorable invitation, though my friends pictured me as winding up a revolver at one ear and a razor at the other."

jealousies and several small fortunes which were involved in this contest, it was as clean and square a fight as ever was staged, and I do not think there is any one who will say otherwise.

The manner in which I fought certainly vindicated me of any charges of "crookedness," and disproved the countless untruths and damaging hints that were bandied about preceding the fight. There have been charges in recent months that Jeffries was doped, and that he entered the ring in a dazed and helpless condition. These charges are absurd, and were raked up by those desiring to revive a controversy which will do neither boxers nor the ring any good. Perhaps they were concocted for no other reason than to please sensation mongers. Certainly, if Jeff was doped, he would have realized it at the time, and even though he might have kept silent as the fight began, hesitating to say anything that would worry his friends, surely he would have said something concerning it after the fight, if for no other reason than to explain his downfall. But he said nothing, and so far as I can learn has not entered the controversy, either to confirm or deny the declarations. Even though Jeff had failed to realize his condition, had he been doped, the expert trainers, sporting authorities, and others about him would have recognized any condition in him resulting from dope or poison of any kind. He was an object of great care and solicitation on the part of those about him. They were watching his condition constantly, and when the hour of the fight arrived, pronounced his condition perfect, because he had been thoroughly examined physically a short time before the bout began. Had he been doped or dazed, I certainly would have recognized such a condition when he got into action. Instead, I found him as alert, energetic and vigorous as any fighter I had faced. There was absolutely no indication of any condition that would impair his mental or physical ability. The charge that he was doped, I must assert, was absolutely unfounded, and I believe Jeff is of like opinion.

That there were those willing and capable of doping either Jeffries or myself, however, I do not doubt. One thing of which I am certain is the fact that an effort was made early in my training to poison me, and had not one of my associates swallowed the poison which was meant for me, the Reno fight might have had an entirely different ending. As it was, Frank Sutton, a member of my training staff, became deathly ill, and was constantly under the care of a doctor. The effect of the poison was just as one might wish, had he planned to disable a boxing contestant, for it left continuous ill effects and it was almost a year before Sutton had recovered, and then only after he had been almost constantly under the care of a physician. The poison was swallowed in a bar-room at the Seal Rock Hotel, San Francisco, where I had established my training quarters. I, myself, and members of my party often went into this particular bar-room for a glass of wine. Sutton, who purchased all my food and superintended its cooking was cautious and watchful. He subjected everything to close scrutiny. On the day he was poisoned his suspicions were aroused and without saying anything to me, he shifted the glasses of wine which had been poured for me and my friends. He got the glass intended for me and it proved to be heavily loaded with something as poor Sutton could well attest for many months afterward. However, he did not slacken in his duties toward me nor relax his vigilance, for, after we had moved to Reno, there were numerous rumors about to the effect that they were going to "get me," and all of us observed the utmost caution in eating, or whenever we were in public. Rumors that gunmen were on my trail were prevalent, and because of this, Governor Dickerson detailed five state rangers to guard me. Happily, no other attempt was made on me; I finished my training, defeated Jeff and left the Nevada town hale and sound.

I feel that I was even in better condition when I stepped into the ring with Jeff than I was on the occasion of the Burns fight. My physical condition was perfect. My training had proceeded to just the right point, and I never felt more fit nor confident than I did on that memorable July 4. My training had begun at Seal Rock but had been interrupted by the stopping of the fight by Governor Gillette. We then moved to Reno, transferred in a special car. We set up our camp at Ricks' roadhouse, and we worked earnestly. In my camp as trainers, sparring partners and seconds were Al Kauffman, Monte Cutler, Kid Cotton, Tom Flannigan, Frank Sutton, Barney Fury, Stanley Ketchel, Bill Delaney and Watson Burns. Bill Little, at the beginning, was my manager and Owen Sighart was business agent.

In my training periods I never maintained a particular chief trainer. I never left it to my trainers to devise methods nor did I look to them for instructions. I had worked out my own system which I believe surpasses all others, and my trainers and others were directed to follow this to the letter. They worked under my directions, and they coöperated in a manner which made our associations pleasant and successful. In developing my system, it was only necessary for me to have substantial and dependable men around me, and in this matter I was exceptionally fortunate in my work at Reno. The men I had with me knew the game. Any one of them was capable as a trainer and any one could have worked a boxer into superb condition. Watson Burns was one of the greatest trainers of all times. Delaney was my chief second, and what a second he was! Others in my corner as seconds were Watson Burns, Harry Foley, Jack Lehay and Barney Fury. Sutton, as I have said, purchased my food and engineered the kitchen. He went to Reno daily, obtaining supplies and never did he buy twice at the same place, if he could help it. He established no permanent purchasing place because he did not intend to give possible food poisoners a chance to do any of their tricks. He watched the kitchen like a hawk. He inspected every food ingredient and all food after it was cooked before I was served.

Every member of my party had confidence in my ability and in my integrity. All thought that I would win the fight and they backed their beliefs to the fullest possible extent. Of all these staunch fellows who aided me in preparing for the fight, none has ever had reason to desert me. All of us, to this day, have remained the closest of friends. Four of them, I regret to say, are dead, but I recall their presence with the tenderest of memories. The four who have gone are Foley, Delaney, Ketchel and Cotton. They, together with those who are still living, made training worth while, and association with them was a privilege and a pleasure. Our lives in training were happy and cheerful. We had good times after some of our initial troubles and disappointments were disposed of, and I suppose that one reason that

Little, Langford and others were sold on the idea that I was going to lie down was because I took life easy; I did not worry much, and sought always to extract for myself and others whatever enjoyment life offered.

So sure was I that I was going to win over Jeff that I lost no opportunity to urge my friends to bet on me, and one time when Hector McKenzie, who was a member of the Jeffries staff came over to my camp, I told him that I knew he was a friend of Jeff as well as a friend of mine, and that I did not wish him to lose any money, and that the best thing for him to do, if he did not wish to bet on me, was to keep his money in his pocket. However, I offered to bet him $5,000 that I would win, to indicate to him my certainty of the outcome of the battle.

Governor Dickerson visited my training camp often and we came to be excellent friends. Our friendship, it proved, was one that was to endure many years. He has always been staunch and loyal, and was one of my closest advisers when I was in prison, where he was superintendent. He took great delight in watching me train. I shall never forget a remark he made one day after watching me spar with Kid Cotton. He said, "I have never seen a man who can whip Jack Johnson as he stands today, and I am forced to bet on him." This observation by the governor followed a bout which I had just finished with Kid Cotton, two days before the fight. I did not wish to box Cotton on that occasion, preferring to polish up with Kauffman, who was more of Jeffries' style and manner. Cotton, however, was anxious to be seen in action that day, because a notable crowd was watching us. The kid was unusually active and aggressive and once butted me on the lower lip with his head which caused me to bleed—something that had never happened to me in boxing. Cotton seemed to be trying to make a grandstand showing, so I gave him his chance. For five rounds, I beat him severely and in the sixth he went down and out. He never was the same Cotton after that. He did not regain his senses until late that afternoon, and once he broke away from those who were caring for him and jumped into an irrigation ditch full of water, and in which he would have drowned, had not Fury and some of the other boys pulled him out. Noting that my lip was bleeding so freely, Governor Dickerson tried to get me to cease training for that day, for, knowing what was in store for me in the next two days, he feared it would not be a good thing for me. The cut caused by Cotton started to bleed again when Jeff hit me, and the fight fans roared with delight, for the thought that Jeff had drawn blood on me was a sign to them that he had the best of me, but it was not Jeff's tap which caused the flow of blood.

A dispute over a poker hand, and a disagreement over a play in a baseball game were the trivial causes of the breach in association between George Little and myself. Never once did we have any misunderstanding over the fight, its terms, or any other business affair as many supposed. It was an unfortunate circumstance, arising, as it did, in the midst of my training and preceding my meeting with Jeffries in a fight that was to be significant in ring annals. It caused much uneasiness on the part of all concerned. It disrupted my camp for a while, and had I been more temperamental it might have had more serious results.

The disagreement over the card game took place on a train on which we were enroute to San Francisco, preparatory to my training. There were three of us in the game, Little, Sighart and myself. Little did not like Sighart and often criticized him. I liked both of them and had confidence in each, and often found it necessary to adjust their differences. In the game Little sat between Sighart and me. During one hand, Little obtained a straight. My hand was no good and I had laid it down. Sighart had a better hand than Little but the latter having more money was able to bet so strong that Sighart was forced to quit. The situation nettled him and he was not in a good mood, feeling, as he did, that Little was deliberately trying to make things unpleasant for him. I dealt the following hand and Sighart opened the pot; Little raised and I staid; Sighart raised Little who again boosted; the pot was raised 15 or 20 times before the draw, the tussle being between Sighart and Little, I being content merely to stay. Little had three kings to start with; Sighart had four jacks and I, although I did no betting had four aces. Sighart drew one card, Little two and I stood pat. Both thought that I had a straight. Little thought that Sighart had tried to fill a flush or straight; he, himself drew his fourth king, and was sure he had both Sighart and myself beat. He raised the bets of Sighart and myself many times. The latter hated to lay down his four jacks, but began to figure that Little had him beat. He accused him of trickery and a hot argument ensued. With the betting, the accusations and quarreling it was more than two hours before the show-down, an unusually long time for deciding the merits of a poker hand. In the quarrel that had taken place, each had accused the other of doing funny things with the deck. I had remained silent throughout the whole proceeding; neither Little nor Sighart had figured me in the game, so when

I won the pot, which contained about $1,500, Little became more enraged than ever and accused Sighart of manipulating the cards so as to give me my four aces. Of course he had done nothing of the sort, but nothing which either Sighart or I could say could convince him that the deal was square. A little while later Little and I clashed again, Sighart having remained out of the pot. When, after considerable raising, I beat Little, he threw his cards down, declaring again that Sighart, who had dealt me the winning hand, was crooked and vowed that he would "get even."

A few days afterwards I hurt my back while training at Seal Rock, and was compelled to take up light exercise. We organized two baseball teams composed of the men in my camp. I was the captain of one and Little of the other. Sighart was playing on my team and during a game one morning, Little and Sighart got into a row over a play at third base. They had come to blows when I stepped in and separated them. After that, Little declared that Sighart would have to go. I told him that he would not—that I would keep him. For a week or more we wrangled over Sighart. Things were in a turmoil and, added to the difficulties occasioned by the Governor's action in preventing the fight, my training was not proceeding very pleasantly or satisfactorily. I told Little that if any one went, it would be he and not Sighart. This was like throwing kerosene on a blaze. Little became vicious and accused me of intending to lie down to Jeffries. At about this time Rickard was visiting me frequently, at which time we talked of how the campaign preceding the fight might be carried on, in order that the public might learn that I was training faithfully, was in good shape, and that none of us had any intention of fooling the public. These talks, into which Little was not invited, made him insanely jealous and he became more and more bitter. He pretended to believe that the talks between Rickard and myself concerned some crooked plan, and accused me of many things. I had borne all his tirades patiently, believing that he did not mean all he had said, but at this juncture I felt I had to get rid of him. After he left my camp, I settled down to real training and things went pleasantly. Flannigan succeeded Little as acting manager.

The day of the fight finally arrived. It was a beautiful one—the weather, excepting for the intense heat, was superb. The atmosphere was clear as crystal, and one could see for miles. More than 25,000 people had gathered to watch the fight, and as I looked about me, and scanned that sea of white faces I felt the auspiciousness of the occasion. There were few men of my own race among the spectators. I realized that my victory in this event meant more than on any previous occasion. It wasn't just the championship that was at stake—it was my own honor, and in a degree the honor of my race. I was well aware of all these things, and I sensed that most of that great audience was hostile to me. These things, while they impressed me with the responsibilities that lay upon me, did not disturb or worry me. I was cool and perfectly at ease. I never had any doubt of the outcome. Outside of a contemplation for a moment of the auspiciousness of the gathering, I was thinking for the most part of getting home. That had been my thought when I crawled through the ropes, and as Fury was tying my gloves I saw in the audience the yardmaster who had charge of the special trains. I sent Fury to ask him to come and speak to me. When he did so, I told him I wanted to leave right after the fight and that I wished him to make arrangements for my immediate departure. He said it would be impossible—that it could not be done. I said it must be done, and that if he would do it I would give him a tip that would make plenty of money for him. He stared at me for a moment, then said that he would get me out on a special.

"Do you mean that?" I asked. He said he did.

"All right, then," I told him. "Bet on me; I am going to win."

I do not know what his winnings were, but he was as good as his word, and two hours after the fight, I was on my way to Chicago on the train which he arranged for me.

I was the first to enter the ring. There was one shady corner and in this I seated myself. Jeff followed a little later with his seconds, and proposed that we toss a coin for the shady corner. I declined to toss, but offered to relinquish the shade to him, an offer which he accepted, and I moved over into the sun. The crowd gave me a very hearty reception, but that given Jeff was twenty times greater than mine. When the fight started Jeff was a 10 to 4 favorite, but in the fourth round I was the favorite by the same odds.

Hardly had a blow been struck when I knew that I was Jeff's master. From the start the fight was mine, and, as I have just observed, the fourth round brought the crowd to a realization that Jeff had little chance to win. He fought in his usual style and I think with as much of his vigor, speed and endurance as ever. If he had not been fit, and if there had been the smallest particle of dope in him, as some have contended, he never could have stood under that hot sun for fifteen rounds withstanding the punishment I gave him. He fought his best. He brought into play some of the old swings and blows for which he had been noted. His brain was working keenly, but he found it almost impossible to get through my defense and at no time did he hurt me. He landed on me frequently but with no effect. He devoted his attention to fighting and did not take much part in the run of conversation which was going on. About all he said, was, once, when I struck him on the head:

"Say, but that's a tough old head," he remarked.

As for me, I took part in the palaver that went on, addressing myself particularly to Jim Corbett, a member of Jeff's training staff, who took occasion to send a few jeering remarks in my direction. I told Corbett to come on in the ring, that I would take him on too. At the same time I was demonstrating, that, contrary to Jim's disparaging remarks, I was putting over a good, fast fight. I hit Jeff at will. There was no place that was beyond my reach, and I landed some stiff jolts on him, but not as stiff as I might have, for I really did not have any desire to punish him unnecessarily. The cheering for Jeff never ceased. The spectators urged him on and gave him every possible encouragement, but their cheering turned to moans and groans when they saw that he was suffering as he was. There came up to me from the ringside gasps of astonishment that turned to cries of pity, and more than once I heard them shout:

"Stop it! Stop it!"

The great crowd cheered Jeffries for his grit and supreme effort and they pitied him in his suffering, but they did not for a moment lose their admiration for him. As for me, they learned that I was not a quitter; they realized that I had not entered into any crookedness, and that Little, Langford and others who had swung much of the betting against me had let them in for a good trimming. However, it was not enough that the fight should be a meritorious one and that the best man had won on his worth or that the entire mill had been clean and square; the crowd was by no means pleased. The "white hope" had failed, and as far as the championship was concerned it was just where it was before the beginning of the fight, except that I had established my rightful claim to it beyond all possible dispute. But from that minute on the hunt for the "white hope" was redoubled, and when it proceeded with so little success other methods were taken to dispose of me, as I have related in former chapters.

The Reno fight probably was attended by more famous sporting men, boxers and promoters than any other. Prominent among them were John L. Sullivan, whose name stands out boldly in world fight records—the first holder of the recognized championship of the world. Hugh McIntosh, the Australian promoter who had backed my fight with Burns was present, and Burns, too, had made a long trip for the occasion. Another promoter present was Jimmy Coffroth. Frank Gotch, the famous wrestler, was in Jeffries' camp. Billy Jordan was the announcer and George Harding was the time-keeper. Bill Lang had come from Australia for the event. Tom McCarey was present and so were Fitzsimmons, Sharkey, Ketchel, Kauffman and hosts of others who had made and were making sport history. There was an army of photographers, newspaper writers, telegraphers. Prominent men from all walks of life had come from England, France, Spain, Mexico, Australia, Canada and every corner of the world to see what they hoped would be the return of the heavy-weight crown to the head of a Caucasian.

Since writing the above, there has come to my attention additional comment concerning the alleged doping of Jeffries for this fight. I have been told that Jeffries himself has said that he was doped and that members of his party have risen to express a similar belief. I am unable to verify the truth of these statements, but I am led to conclude that such men as Bob Edgren, James Corbett, Sharkey, Choynski and other notables in sport circles who were with Jeffries at the time, all said to be experts and authorities upon points relating to a boxer's condition and capabilities, certainly had a part in misleading the public if, knowing that Jeffries was in no condition to enter the ring on July 4, 1910, because of the effects of drugs, they permitted him to attempt the fight. I am sure that their claim to expertness and trustworthiness must be considerably weakened if what they say is true and they knew it on the day of the fight; and they must have known it that day, for certainly there would be no way of discovering it after the fight— several years afterwards, at least. About the only dope which Jeffries suffered from was that administered by myself in the form of jabs and uppercuts to the jaw.

# CHAPTER XI

## CHALLENGERS

REPOSING in a Paris bank are something like 300,000 francs under court supervision, 250,000 of which belongs to me; the other 50,000 belongs to Mike Moran, an American boxer now living in the West. This bank account equivalent to about $60,000, together with interest, since June, 1914, Moran and I expect to have paid over to us within a short time. The money represents the gate receipts of a fight which took place in Paris between Mike and me in the above month and year. It was placed in the bank at the direction of a court in which an attachment was brought against the gate by McCarthy, an American publicity man, who obtained the order following a disagreement between him, Moran's manager and myself, a disagreement occasioned by McCarthy's greediness in trying to obtain more money than his contract with us provided for. Pending a decision by the court, the war came on, delaying matters at first; later McCarthy died and court action was further delayed. Information which recently reached us is to the effect that the money is to be paid to us shortly.

My fight with Moran was for the championship of the world, and because of that fact and other circumstances connected with it, it is one of more than passing interest. I was at the time a fugitive, which accounts for the fight taking place in Paris. Moran had ambitions to try for the title, and his manager Dan McKetrick of Pittsburgh opened negotiations with me.

Acting as my own manager, I accepted Moran's challenge and made the necessary arrangements in the French capital for the meeting. This fight, while by no means the greatest, was one of the most interesting of my career, and for some reason I recall it vividly—more vividly than any other similar contest.

I trained earnestly and faithfully for this fight, because I knew that Moran was no commonplace contender, and I desired that, taking place as it did in a foreign capital, it should be a successful and satisfying public event, because boxing is a popular sport in France, and spectators like to get their money's worth. Only a few were aware of the intensity with which I trained, because most of my training was done under cover. It was said of me that I did not take the fight seriously and there was considerable doubt as to whether or not I would be in condition. It was my custom to arise at 4:30 o'clock in the morning and hit the road for a long and hard sprint. It was at this time that I discovered that France was preparing for war, though the public was unaware of the approaching conflict. Each morning along the route which I followed in my road work, I saw large masses of French soldiers maneuvering. It was said they were only engaged in periodical training, but there were signs in their movements which caused me to know that there was something more serious astir. On returning to my quarters, I would relate to members of my party what I had observed and many times declared that France was preparing for war with Germany. My assertions were laughed at and much joking was indulged in at my expense over what was termed my unnecessary alarm.

One morning while taking my usual run, I met a German who engaged me in conversation. He manifested deep interest in me and the approaching fight, and asked permission to visit my quarters. He lost no time in presenting himself. He inquired concerning my morning road work, asked about the hours and the routes which I took. These questions apparently were harmless and I answered them unsuspectingly. He next asked permission to accompany me on the runs, and I assented to his proposal. He went with me several mornings. It was a terrible ordeal for him. He could not keep up with me and spent most of his time and breath begging me to go slower. I could not accommodate him on this point because I was eager to carry on my training to the utmost. I was in splendid condition and, despite his appeals, I traveled at top speed leaving him far behind. He would come up panting and exhausted when I stopped, but he was game and tried hard to cover the ground with me. He soon dropped out of the early morning trips, however, and began a program of questioning seeking to find out what I knew about the movements, numbers and intentions of the French troops which I had observed. I told him little because I knew little. I afterwards learned that he was a spy in the employ of the German government.

As I continued my training, neither Moran nor the public knew much of my movements. I would finish my work by 7 o'clock in the morning and rest until 9 o'clock. I would then have breakfast and later I would make a round of the cafés, loiter along the streets or visit with idling friends. My apparent idleness caused everyone to believe that I was giving little attention to training and I frequently was reproached by those concerned in my success for my laziness or lack of interest.

Meanwhile, Moran was doing much hard training and in a manner which impressed the public with his earnestness and skill.

One afternoon when I was engaged in ball punching McKetrick, Moran's manager appeared at my training quarters accompanied by McCarthy whom he introduced as an American publicity man who had lost most of his money in Paris, and who was seeking some means of recuperating his fortune. I always was ready to aid Americans, especially when they were in distress on foreign shores, and when McKetrick suggested that we might engage McCarthy as a publicity agent for the fight I readily assented, and we signed a contract giving McCarthy 5 per cent of the gross gate receipts.

The arrangement was a satisfactory one all around and none appeared better pleased than McCarthy himself. All plans for the fight proceeded smoothly. McCarthy did good work. The public was deeply aroused over the battle and the advance sale of tickets was huge. More than 25,000 spectators attended the fight. When McCarthy noted the exceptional flow of gate money he became dissatisfied and sought to change his contract to provide for a payment of 10 per cent instead of 5 per cent. I would not agree to this, and I was backed up in my stand by McKetrick. We engaged in a row of considerable bitterness, the upshot of which was the resignation of McCarthy followed immediately by his attachment of the entire gate receipts, a step which, as I have previously related, tied up the proceeds of the fight.

Moran and I fought twenty rounds. I do not believe that he hit me a half-dozen times. From the tenth to the twentieth, I cut him to pieces. During the first ten rounds I made little effort in the fight. The public thought my training had been insufficient and that my condition was poor. Moran thought I was doing my best and figured that if he could stay ten rounds he would beat me. But in the eleventh round, I unlimbered and began punching harder and faster than ever, much to Moran's surprise. I literally slashed him to ribbons. The crowd livened up and yelled with glee, because the French certainly like to see athletes punish each other, and flowing blood to them is the sign of something worth while. When the fight ended several doctors sprang into the ring to examine Moran and give him first aid. He was under the doctors' care for more than two weeks.

I believe that on the night of that fight, Moran was in the best condition of his life, and that he could have whipped any white man in the world. He put up a wonderful fight and struggled every minute to land a telling punch on me, but in vain. I also believe that the fight was one of the best Paris fight fans ever witnessed. As for myself, I was in splendid condition mentally and physically and got much entertainment out of Moran and the crowd. As I write this, I am recalling in the most vivid manner every detail of that fight. I can see myself jabbing with my left, uppercutting, occasionally stopping right swings from Moran and sending my right to his jaw. I can hear myself kidding Moran and telling him what a nice fellow he was. I told him it did not look right for him to have black eyes and a scarred face. He didn't waste much time kidding back, but kept coming at me with blows intended to be wicked, but all of which failed to connect. Once, he slipped me a glancing punch and the crowd screamed with joy. At this time, I dumbfounded Moran and the spectators by stepping back and joining with the spectators in the applause, pounding my gloved hands with all the energy I could and raising my voice in the shouts of approval. As the fight went on, I carried on a conversation with McKetrick, asking him when he intended to sail for the United States, and whether or not he wished to become my manager. I told Moran he was a great fighter—that he was putting up a great fight, but that he would never again be the fighter he was that night. When the fight ended I did not bear a scratch and was not in the least fatigued. I went to the dressing room, donned my evening clothes and went to a dinner and dance. Moran went into the fight confident that he would win, and bet heavily upon himself, basing his confidence on his belief that I had not trained sufficiently, and on the further contingency that I had broken my left arm in a fight a while before with Jim Johnson, a tough boxer from the States.

The crowd before which we fought was, I believe, the best dressed I ever saw gathered about a boxing ring. Everyone in attendance was in evening clothes, with the exception of the Dolly sisters who then were appearing in a Paris theater, and who had come to the fight because of their former acquaintance with me, when I appeared with them on the American stage in a fifteen-weeks' engagement. Moran and McKetrick left Paris shortly after the fight and just preceding the war. I never saw the former again until May, 1926, when we met in Juarez, Mexico, where we had a jolly meeting, talked over the Paris fight and discussed our chances of getting the money held in the Paris bank.

My fight with Stanley Ketchel, who aspired to the heavyweight championship took place in Colma, Calif., October 16, 1909. Ketchel was an excellent fighter in the ring and a fine fellow out of the ring. He was, at the time of our contest, world's champion middleweight boxer. To my mind, he was far too small and light ever to have defeated a heavyweight, but the fact that he was game enough to try it proved his courage and confidence. Those who saw the fight or the pictures know that I played with Ketchel as I liked and that I refrained from punishing him any more than was necessary. I write this portion of my autobiography with regret and sorrow because Ketchel is dead, and he was one of my best friends and one whom I admired for his many excellent qualities. Because he is dead, I shall try to write not only truthfully but most respectfully of Ketchel's part in my life. In making the match with Ketchel I had a clever fellow to deal with in the person of Willis Britt, Ketchel's manager. I was my own manager in this event and between Britt and myself there was considerable argument over percentages. However, Ketchel was a great drawing card and I knew it. I knew that he and I together could draw a record gate. Because of this I did not wish to pass up the opportunity afforded by this match because of a few cents difference in percentages, and I finally assented to a percentage for Ketchel which was greater than I would have granted any other living fighter. I figured that I must get a large proportion of my money out of the pictures and was determined to make the fight an interesting and exciting one. Both Ketchel and I were trained to the minute and were in excellent trim for the contest. With the ability he had, I knew he would make a good showing and I, being so much larger, decided to give him a chance for the purpose of affording the spectators as much thrill and entertainment as possible. I was hoping for something of a sensational nature and tried to devise a plan to that end.

On the day of the fight, I started in my car with my seconds and personal party to the Colma arena. I was driving a six-ninety Thompson Flier and traveling at a rate of speed that enabled me to pass Ketchel and his party who were going to the ring in a white Lozier, at that time considered America's classiest cars. He was going 62 miles an hour he told me later. Despite the speed I was driving I was busily thinking how I could make the fight picturesque, and a plan occurred to me. This plan I did not divulge to any of my party though I told Bob Armstrong, one of my sparring partners, that if he should see me down in a certain round he need not get excited. We arrived at the arena 20 minutes before the fight and found that every ticket had been sold. We caught several men on the gate knocking down on us. We made them shake loose their cash and put it in the cash box, fired them off the gate and replaced them with others.

Once in the ring I looked about me and was surprised to find that every possible space that could hold a human body was filled. A few minutes afterward Ketchel entered the ring and I turned my attention from the crowd to him. I looked him over as he sat in his corner, and saw a man whom I recognized as a great fighter. I figured to myself that Ketchel was a good puncher and a game man, and that I must carry on the fight in a way that would make the pictures snappy and worth seeing. I decided that I would take him along for several rounds and let him make a good showing, so that the spectators would not tire of the fight. However, I did not propose to let him hurt me. I followed this plan throughout the fight and as it neared the end, I had Ketchel well in hand

and could do with him as I wished. He sent over a punch which landed on my jaw. It did not hurt nor disconcert me. My brain had been working rapidly—so rapidly that I recognized this to be a clean cut blow with apparently much force back of it. I said to myself, "Now's your time! Now's your time! Here's your chance," and so I hit the canvas. All the time I was watching Ketchel and the referee. I was watching the latter so that he would not count me out and I watched Ketchel so that he would be in the position I wished when I arose. In order to do this, it was necessary for me to get up at a certain angle. It would cause him to move into the position I desired. As I got to my feet, I pretended to be groggy, but in reality I was ready to deliver the knockout. Ketchel rushed me with determination to put me out. I met him with a murderous blow that put him out instead. It was a right uppercut and the fight was over. Stanley lost several teeth, and when I returned to the dressing room I found one of his teeth embedded in my glove. After the fight we became fast friends and continued so until the day of his death. He was a member of my boxing party when I fought Jeffries and was an able assistant. When he was shot to death by a cowardly assassin on the farm of Colonel Dickinson in Missouri, there was no one who grieved more than I, because I admired him and counted him as one of my most valued friends.

# CHAPTER XII

## THE FRAME-UP FOR FREEDOM

DEFINITE arrangements for my fight with Willard began when Jack Curley came to London to talk it over with me. The selection of Willard came about in the process of hunting the "white hope." The result of the fight ended that search, which had been carried on so intensely and bitterly that it had caused me much trouble and sorrow, because of the persecution to which I was subjected. On his arrival in London, Curley asked me if I meant business in meeting Willard. I told him I certainly did and that he would not find it difficult to make terms with me. The first night of Curley's stay in London, we visited the Coliseum where Oscar Ash and Lillie Braton were appearing. We did not talk shop that night. The next day we went to lunch and the preliminaries began, and in the evening at dinner we began to talk more freely. I told Curley to put all the cards on the table and to deal from the top of the deck. I had known him a long time. We had been close friends and had met in previous mutually satisfactory business deals. At one time in my life, when I was in serious trouble, he had stood loyally by me. As a result of this, I had the utmost confidence in him.

He frankly told me that if I lost the fight to Willard I could return to the United States without being molested. He said that I would be able to engage in a prosperous occupation and would gain new friends and please old acquaintances who were anxious to see me comfortably and peacefully settled down at home. These hints were inducements of course, but the greatest inducement of all was the opportunity it offered me to see my mother, for all who know me and who have read about me, know that whatever other failings I may have had, the love I had for my mother was so deep and sincere that I would have done anything to end the separation between us. After Curley had talked a while, explaining the chances I would have and mentioning my mother several times, I became more anxious than ever to get back home. After that first conversation with him, I did not care any more for the title of world's champion than a child does for the stick from which the lollypop has vanished. In fact, I despised it.

Curley explained that Frazee and Webber, amusement promoters, were associated with him in arranging with me to meet Willard. The fight, he said, would be held in Juarez, Mexico, and Villa, the revolutionary bandit leader who then controlled northern Mexico would finance the fight. Curley remained in London a week or so, and when he departed we had reached an agreement, as far as I was concerned, which would give Willard the championship and permit me to return home. He gave me sufficient money to defray transportation expenses to Mexico and I set about making preparations for going to the scene of the proposed fight. I did not tell my wife nor Gus, my nephew, that I had agreed to lose the fight, but pretended that I had entered into the deal with the hope and expectation of winning.

Taking our leave of London, we embarked for Rio de Janeiro early in 1914. We made a brief stay on our arrival at the South American port, and then departed for Buenos Aires, where we remained for six weeks and where I put on several boxing exhibitions. When it came time for us to leave the latter city, we found great difficulty in arranging passage for a trip back to Rio de Janeiro, and after much search were compelled to board a freight vessel which took us to Barbados in the West Indies where my party remained three weeks, and where I did much exhibition boxing and made many friends.

It was our intention to go from Barbados to Vera Cruz or Tampico, Mexico, but owners of vessels and crews were dubious about venturing far out to sea because of the submarine danger which they believed existed, because of Germany's threats to carry on "ruthless sea warfare." We finally persuaded the owner of a small sailing vessel to attempt a trip to Havana, Cuba, a port which we reached after a hazardous trip during which we were driven by a gale and nearly wrecked. After I reached Havana, I learned from the newspapers that it was the intention of Carranza, president of Mexico, to capture me if I sought to land either at Vera Cruz or Tampico, and turn me over to the United States authorities, whereupon I got into communication with Curley, who had gone to Juarez to arrange for the fight. After several cable messages, I induced him to come to Havana. Upon his arrival, I explained my predicament and sought to have the scene of the Willard fight changed to Havana, because I was eager to go through with my part of the bargain. Then I intended to surrender to the United States, but I did not wish to risk capture by Carranza, because I foresaw that such a circumstance would involve me in official red tape and delays which I was in no mind to contend with.

On his arrival in Havana, Curley said that Frazee, Webber and himself had made arrangements for me to return to the United States if I lost to Willard, but first I was to take the films of the fight and exhibit them in South America and Europe, which sections of the globe were to be my exclusive territory. I collected the fight percentage due me just before the fight, but an additional percentage, which Willard's managers owed me if I lived up to my agreement to lie down, was not paid until the fight was almost over. They tried hard to renege on payments to me and even went so far as to try and deprive me of the films which were to be given me, according to contract. Pictures of the fight were made by Mace, and when I learned that the situation was not ripe for my return to the United States, I immediately left Havana for London. I was told when my boat was ready to leave that the films were not in readiness but that they would be sent to me in London as soon as they were finished. I waited for the pictures several weeks and when they did not arrive, I cabled to Curley asking why they had not been sent. He replied that they were on the way. I watched eagerly for their arrival, and when they did arrive, I was astounded to find that they were blank—that they never had been on a spool. I cabled demanding an explanation and in reply was told that the deception or mistake was due to Mace, the maker of the films.

This turn of affairs enraged me and I started other inquiries by cable, the result of which, among other things, brought me the information that Curley and his associates had made no move whatever to provide for my return to the United States. The failure of the films to arrive had not caused me to lose faith in my supposed friends. I tried to believe in them and to charge the delay in the films to other causes, but when I found that they had not kept their word in paving the way for me to return home I became not only cognizant of the fact that I had been flim-flammed but that I was up against a pretty raw deal. Therefore, I kept silent, but was not inactive. Inquiring at the office of the American Express Company, I learned that a film of the Willard-Johnson fight was being shipped to London from the United States. I knew that some plot was under way and I hired detectives to trace and watch the shipment. When it arrived I stayed close around the express company's office, knowing that some one would call for it.

I was not mistaken in this. A young man named A. Weil, who now lives in Chicago, appeared on the scene to claim the films. When they were transferred to him, I snatched them from him and obtained possession, though not until after a heated argument and various attempts to get them from me had taken place. I contracted with Barker & Company, one of the largest film firms in England to make prints of the films, and these I put on exhibition throughout England. I also sold the rights to the pictures to a South American company and with the proceeds from this sale and the display of the pictures in the United Kingdom was able to realize very satisfactory returns—returns which were ample enough to make me feel somewhat repaid for the manner in which Curley and his partners had bilked me. I also sold the Australian rights to the pictures to Rufe Nailor.

Preceding the fight with Willard, I did no serious training. I engaged in a few boxing exhibitions and did a few "strong man" stunts, such as pulling against horses and permitting a horse to stand on my stomach. This was about the extent of my training. I had no wish to undergo the ordeal of strict training knowing as I did how the fight was to terminate. Mrs. Johnson, my nephew Gus, my sparring partners and friends were curious and alarmed over my failure to train properly and several times demanded to know what my object was in being so indifferent. I boxed occasionally with Bob Armstrong, Sam McVey and some other American boxers whom I had previously fought in America, but as I always had been able to box rings around all of them, they never knew whether or not I was in shape.

On one occasion Mahoney, an American contractor who had played a big part in the Spanish-American War, and who then was living in Havana overheard me talking to Willard and repeating "Hit me! Come on, hit me!" I was then a big favorite in the betting. What Mahoney heard caused him to take quick leave of the arena and re-enter by another way, when he laid a big bet on Willard. He won a big sum of money, of course. It just happens that today Mahoney is a very close friend of mine. I have visited Cuba three times since the Willard fight, and on each occasion Mahoney has met me and been my host.

I did not tell Mrs. Johnson I was going to lose the fight until a few moments before I entered the ring. Curley had paid me my fight percentage before I left my home. No one knew that the money was there, and I employed four policemen to guard the home, though they did not know that it was because of the money, and with the understanding that they merely were to watch the premises. I instructed Mrs. Johnson to sit at the ringside and watch the fight; that there was more money due me, and until this money was paid to me, I would not let the fight take the course agreed upon. Delay in paying this money was due to the incomplete count of gate receipts, which was under way when the fight started. Mrs. Johnson was to signal me when she had received the additional money, and I was to signal her so that she might leave the ringside. The fight was originally intended to end in the tenth round, but when that round arrived the money had not been paid. It was nearing the twenty-sixth round when the money was turned over to Mrs. Johnson. I had specified that it should be in $500 bills in order that the package should be small and the amount quickly counted. After examining it she gave me the signal. I replied that everything was O.K. by a pre-arranged sign and she departed. In the twenty-sixth round I let the fight end as it did. I felt very sorry for Mrs. Johnson, to have to relinquish the belt, but I was not sorry that I had lost the championship—or rather permitted another to attain it. On the contrary, I was happy, because I hopefully looked forward to my speedy return to the United States, where I would again be with my old friends and above all, with my mother. It was this expectation of my return to my native land, my friends and my mother that determined my part in the historic Johnson-Willard fight and explains why and how I lost it. *

---

* There is some discrepancy here. Johnson publicly said he threw the fight, but most boxing experts did not believe him. They said he was out of shape. The promise that Johnson could return to the United States without facing the prison term proved to be untrue. And Johnson never received the $50,000 he said he did.

# CHAPTER XIII

## Reflections on Life and on Living

EVERY second of our lives is devoted to battling against death. For the most part we wage the battle unconsciously. We are unaware of the conflict as long as we have good health and possess our faculties unimpaired. It is only when illness overtakes us that we are reminded of the potential dangers of disease. Even when we feel in the best of health and spirits, and the body is functioning normally, resistance to death is being carried on constantly. Nature carries on the fight regardless of our interest. Most of us are disinterested, assuming that nature will do her part without our aid or attention. We become neglectful and what is worse, deliberately set obstacles in nature's way making her battle for life much harder and often futile. If we would learn to co-operate with nature in the maintenance of health and bodily vigor, disease would be surprisingly reduced, we would be more efficient physically and mentally and life would perhaps be prolonged scores of years. The process of co-operation is so simple and easy that it is astounding that we are so shamelessly and criminally neglectful. The average man knows less about the functions of his body and the proper manner of maintaining it than he does about his automobile. Men know how to build up and maintain big fortunes but they do not know how to maintain their health—the greatest fortune of all. They are authorities in finance and commerce, but woefully ignorant and neglectful in matters pertaining to their bodies and their health. They wage great contests in the social and industrial world, but permit their bodies to bear the burden of health maintenance unaided.

Whether we admit it or not, death has the advantage over life. It creeps in in many ways. It may find its hold on the body because of some apparently inconsequential condition which, if resisted at the time, or better still prevented by proper care of the body, would have presented a more formidable resistance to death. Since death is the aggressor, life should have an even break—a break that can be provided by the owner of the body if he will give it the protection and the health that is due it. The fight between life and death is to the finish, and death ultimately is the victor, but its coming can be delayed many years. Life can be made to last scores of years beyond the present-day average, and even if it were impossible to lengthen out the years, one can achieve more happiness and success throughout the ordinary lifetime if he keeps his body strong and healthy.

The greatest and most harmful fallacy current among men today is that pertaining to age. The belief that one must slow down when he gets out of the thirties and retire from the pleasures and activities of life when he gets into the fifties is rank superstition. We worship the glory of youth, and we should, because youth is wonderful. But youth is by no means the fulfillment of life. It is the stepping stone, the means and the source of reaching better things in life, of making what we call the middle-age and old-age periods more beautiful and successful—and more wonderful even than youth; for if, in youth, men and women set about building up their bodies and constructing health defenses, they cannot only delay the coming of death, but they will find their old age worth living. They will come nearer to attaining the ideals of happiness and contentment.

The organs, muscles, nerves and all parts and faculties of the body should be properly exercised and trained. Inaction is a deadly foe of health and life, but mere training and exercising is not all. These will prove insufficient if we fail to give attention to right living. The people of the world today, Americans in particular, are not living as they should. They are victims of both over and under-indulgence. They are extremists and are plunging foolishly and blindly into life without knowing or caring what they are doing. The things which are done for the good of health are out-balanced by the things which are enemies to health. The American people are lazy and neglectful in caring for their health— lazy because they fail to take proper exercise and neglectful because they overlook simple and yet very important rules which nature has established and which must be observed if life and health are to have fullest expression.

In America there are thousands of unnecessary deaths yearly from heart trouble, which, in some instances can be traced to lack of exercise and improper eating; there are countless other deaths from the same cause due to over-exercise. Hence my conviction that Americans are extremists. Heart troubles, resulting from over-exercise, are prevalent among athletes, many of whom die at early ages from heart afflictions due to severe strain. There are deaths, too, from overwork, where the overwork is of such a nature as to either strain the muscles or vital organs or disrupt the nervous system. But the most prolific cause of ill health, probably, is improper eating, which induces disarrangement of the digestive system.

When this important function is interrupted or arrested other diseases find an easy foot-hold.

Over-eating by a normal person, who is not engaged in physical activities which absorb his surplus energy, frequently causes "gas" in the stomach which is not only very uncomfortable but which may become dangerous. Sometimes what is diagnosed as stomach trouble or indigestion is in reality heart trouble, that organ being susceptible to conditions reflected from the stomach. I do not mean by these vague hints that all normal persons should diet, but every person, no matter how young or healthy, should eat with care and select foods which have the most important nutrient qualities. Young and healthy persons can "eat almost anything," but it is not desirable for them to do so, because, while such aptitudes for eating in youth may not show immediate ill results, they are likely to appear in later years. Even allowing that it is permissible to eat anything, there is one other danger that should be remembered and that is over-eating; no matter what the particular food may be, there is danger of not only putting a strain on the digestive organs, but when large quantities of food are allowed to enter the stomach the digestive juices or chemical fluids which the digestive organs secrete, for the assimilation of food, are likely to become exhausted, and the time will come when the food will be only partly digested. This means that the blood will be cheated of its required nutrition, unabsorbed materials remaining in the stomach as waste and create complications. The poisons created will be distributed throughout the system and the intestines will be compelled to undergo harmful strain in helping to dispose of the waste that has accumulated.

In the present highly developed civilized age when

modern inventions have made it possible for man to perform nearly every service automatically, the tendency toward physical inaction is more accentuated than ever. Modern transportation methods have reduced natural means of locomotion to a minimum. The ever-present automobile, and other means of travel, tempt man to cover even the shortest distances without using the facilities which nature provides for this purpose. For this reason alone, it is more necessary than ever that we should turn to ways of bodily development by regular and scientific methods. The high pressure at which we live, and the constant effort to make profitable use of our time, detracts from natural body functioning. In our hurry, we gulp down our meals, permitting large and solid pieces of food to enter the stomach without proper mastication. The food thus enters the stomach without being subjected to thorough chewing, for which purpose nature has provided us with teeth, and is denied the benefits of the saliva especially secreted in the mouth, shifting greater responsibility on the digestive apparatus and adding to the strain of organs which should be permitted to do their work with greater ease if longevity is to be considered as worth while. We should spend more time at our meals. If, however, they must be eaten hurriedly, then the food should be small in quantity and light in content. One should learn to govern the appetite, because the desire for food often is not the body's signal for the need of food. It too often is merely the wish to indulge in the pleasure of taste gratification, in the course of which we consume more food than is required and eat many things which are injurious to the stomach, and compel the digestive equipment to do unnecessary work in assimilating food that has no nutritive qualities.

It is impossible to prescribe a general diet that will meet the needs of all. What is good for one person may be harmful to another. I have found it a safe rule for the healthy person, however, to eat what he likes as long as he does not go to extremes. But it is foolhardy to eat any food that does not furnish the necessary nutrition, just because one likes it. The intelligent man or woman can, by observing the results of their eating, arrive at a workable idea of what does and does not agree with them. There is one thing obvious in America and England—and that is the fact that the consumption of meat in both countries is so huge that it may account for much of the ill health that prevails. For the sake of health and the preservation of our digestive organs, it may be advisable to eat less meat. There are so many other foods that are just as palatable and decidedly less harmful with as great and sometimes greater nutritive value, that it is not only unnecessary but foolish to eat as much meat as we do.

Fruits and vegetables should occupy a more prominent place on American menus. In these are to be found all the food constituents needed and they are more easily disposed of in the stomach, because they possess, in addition to their nutritive qualities, other valuable ingredients for the organism. One of the greatest of foods, and one which scientific investigation has proved to be almost ideal, is the banana. If it were generally known what a splendid food this is, its consumption would be greatly increased, food bills would be cut down and our health would greatly improve. This fruit is one of the most important heat and energy-producing foods and it contains some of the essential food elements required by the human body.

I do not wish to appear technical nor pretend to scientific knowledge in the field of diet, but I may call attention to the now well-known fact that the principal food nutrients consist of carbohydrates, proteins, inorganic salts and vitamins. These elements are required by the body for the production of heat and energy; for the restoration of tissue lost through wear and tear; for growth and for the protection of the body against disease. The fuel, or energy value of food, is calculated from its power to produce heat when burned. The unit of measure in food values is the calory, or to be more explicit, a healthy man weighing, say, 150 pounds, performing the work of the average man, requires a food intake of about 3,000 calories daily. An analysis of the banana by the United States department of agriculture shows that this fruit contains 73.3 percent of water; 1.3 percent protein; 0.6 percent fat; 22.0 percent carbohydrates and 0.8 percent mineral matter and that the number of calories per pound contained in the banana is 460. This authentic test should be sufficient to convince any one intent on obtaining a good, all-around food that the banana is unexcelled.

I demonstrated to my own satisfaction long ago that the banana possessed a wonderful nutritive value, but I am glad to say that I do not base my praise of the banana upon my own ideas or observations. Besides the government test, many food and scientific authorities declare the banana to be all that I have claimed for it. Among these, the following may be quoted: Prof. J. Russell Smith of Columbia University in a book on the "World's Food Resources," says:

"The possibilities of the banana as a food resource for the temperate zone have only begun to be developed."

Prof. Samuel C. Prescott of the Massachusetts Institute of Technology writes:

"The fact that bananas may be obtained in abundance throughout the year, that they may be shipped for long distances under suitable conditions without being impaired in any way, that they may be used as a fruit or as a vegetable, cooked or raw, in their normal form or dried as a powder, shows clearly that in this remarkable fruit we have an adjunct to our dietary which should not be overlooked."

Sir James Crichton-Browne, a famous British physician and Fellow of the Royal Society, has this to say:

"Extended experience of the banana has deepened my conviction in its food value. It is a great boon to the masses of our people and, while retaining its place on the dessert table of the rich, has found its way into the hands of the poor. Its portability, palatability and digestibility are immense advantages."

Adequate rest and sleep are factors which enter into the maintenance of health, but unfortunately, we in America, in our high ambitions and our multitudinous interests, are inclined to rob our bodies of these essentials. They are as important as proper selection and eating of food. There are some persons who do not require much sleep, and there are others who require much above the average. However, eight or nine hours of good sleep are absolutely necessary for the welfare of the body and the brain. Sufficient sleep is a great healer of bodily ills; it restores spent energy and promotes contentment. When the brain is tired the whole body is sluggish. Many people who have headaches wonder at the cause. In many instances, headaches may be traced to weariness or disarranged functioning of the stomach or liver, kid-

neys and the brain. In most cases, headache is a sign
that the blood is not circulating as it should or is lacking
in some of its elements, a condition which physicians call
anaemia. If an aching head is chronic, one should consult a physician, but if they are spasmodic a little observation will soon reveal the cause, and a remedy in some
cases will be found in breathing plenty of fresh air.
This is a simple cure, but it is nevertheless efficacious.
A brisk walk in the air, if one arises with a headache,
usually disperses it. Disease germs thrive in the blood
and find their way into this important bodily element
often through lack of pure air or from food wastes in
the stomach. Just how far good air will go in annihilat-
ing germs may be realized when it is remembered that
some germs will live for hours in hot or decayed solutions, but will die instantaneously when brought into contact with air and sunlight. Persons with lung or stomach
troubles should always sleep where there is plenty of
fresh air and sunshine.

Another condition detrimental to good health is surplus flesh. Persons carrying excess flesh are easily
fatigued. By taking adequate physical exercise before
one becomes too fleshy, other organic complications can
be prevented. Exercise also improves the breathing
functions, and when one breathes freely and copiously
the lungs absorb sufficient air to keep the blood pure,
which acts to combat the major diseases of the body.

One of the best forms of exercise in the world is walking. It brings most of the muscles into action and facili-
tates breathing of fresh, pure air, especially if one gives
his attention to the process of walking and throws energy
and pep into it. If one is hindered from walking either
because of lack of time or a place to walk, the medicine

ball becomes a great adjunct for exercise, because it can be used easily within doors; it affords possibilities for energetic and snappy activity and does not require much time. Pulleys also are within the reach of the average person and can be installed in any home, but best of all for home exercising is the punching ball and the man using this thirty minutes a day will always be in fine physical condition. Women have not taken to the punching ball, because it may seem that it is not in accordance with their needs or aptitudes, but I would advise women to make use of the punching ball as well as men.

This ball will make both men and women fit. It not only exercises most of the muscles but it makes one mentally alert; it makes them think quickly, and it is a wonderful training for the eye. Use of the ball is easily learned. It is an economical method and can be placed in any home. Besides its contribution to physical vigor, it will be found of great value to the automobile driver, because as I have said, it trains the eye and promotes quick thinking. Spalding & Company, makers of sporting goods, have such equipment as I have mentioned. They have a small punching ball apparatus that can be installed in any room; the pulleys, such as they offer, may be placed either in the bedroom or bathroom or wherever one may wish. After a few weeks' use either of the punching ball, or pulleys, one will find a wonderful change in one's condition. Their users will be agreeably surprised at the way in which their health and bodily strength will be improved.

For the man or woman who does not like the punching ball or pulleys I would suggest one-pound dumb-bells. Gymnasiums have prescribed methods of using dumb-bells, but no particular movement is necessary.

One may devise his own methods, as long as brisk motional exercise is carried on with them. With them one may engage in shadow boxing, feinting and skipping. Women can go through these exercises as well as men and they will find that, after a few attempts, their physical condition will not only improve but that they will derive keen pleasure out of the performance. The use of the dumb-bells regularly will improve digestion, aid in proper breathing, promote agility of the arms and legs, stir sluggish blood to coursing through the veins as it should and give the appetite a zest that not only will make foods more palatable but more easily digestible. The punching ball, pulleys or dumb-bells can be used by all men, women and children, old and young.

For those who have weak stomachs or whose stomachs have suffered in early days from abuse, I would suggest careful dieting until the stomach tissues have been restored to good condition, inflammation is removed and the digestive organs have had a chance to recuperate. Briefly I would outline the following foods:

For breakfast: A pot of tea in the morning, not too strong nor too hot; crackers or buttered toast and a couple of eggs in any style desired provided they are not hard-boiled.

Lunch: Beef or chicken broth, or a light vegetable soup with fruits, peas or corn.

Dinner: Many people have a habit of eating heavily in the evening. This is one of our most harmful practices as far as eating is concerned. Heavy meals require much time for digestion and if they are not thoroughly digested before one retires, a sleepless, restless night is likely to ensue and one will arise fatigued the next morning. For those desiring or requiring a diet, I would recommend that they dispense with meat, and eat instead fish or fowl. They should have a variety of vegetables but should not indulge in them heavily.

Orange juice is a popular morning drink, but for my part I prefer it just before retiring, because I believe it has an excellent effect in providing action for the stomach as one sleeps, and I am sure one will derive better results from it when taken just before bedtime than when it is used for a morning drink.

I have said much about bananas as a food factor and I would again remind my readers to make good use of them. The housewife, if she will consult a good cook book, will learn that there are many ways to serve bananas and that they not only make a palatable and nutritious food, but will aid her many times in planning menus for any hour of the day. They have a place on the table morning, noon and night.

I would be lax in my advice concerning foods and eating, were I to neglect mentioning buttermilk. This is a food element that may be consumed by the strong and healthy, the weak and ill with equally good effects. Those with weak stomachs will find buttermilk healthful and all will find it refreshing, thirst-quenching and tissue building.

I have been asked many times what I thought of the effects of alcohol on the system. Anyone knows that alcohol taken in excess is injurious just as a good many other things are. But when there is not an overindulgence in alcohol I believe that instead of being harmful it is beneficial. Many of our foods are alcoholic in content, and alcohol is a required element in promoting proper digestion—so greatly required that it is one of the functions of the digestive system to manufacture it.

It is heat producing and invigorating. A glass of wine, not too cold, is an excellent aid to weak stomachs and I believe good beer in moderation is health building. However, I raise my voice with the loudest in protesting against the prevailing alcoholic drinks now flowing in America. They are poisonous and dangerous.

It might seem that I, who have devoted nearly all the years of my life to boxing and the severest form of athletic work, who once held the world's heavyweight boxing championship, and who has engaged in more ring contests than any other heavyweight boxer—am stepping out of my role, when I presume to turn my attention for the moment to subjects that have no relation to my profession, subjects which in fact are far removed from the stern business of pugilism. But even a boxer must come in contact with life and its many problems. His is a business that permits him to rub against humanity in all its forms; he sees the high and the low spots, and feels the bumps of the rough places and the delight of the smooth ones. When he has lived as I have, on the edge of two of the greatest eras of world history, and has, because of the peculiar twists of fate to which I have been subjected, been thrown into all classes of society; when he has felt the stings of life as I have and also gloried in the triumphs that were mine, he comes to know many things and to think of many things that are not in the category of sports and boxing.

When I first began to sit up and take notice of things and to cast about for something to occupy my efforts and attention, there still lived in the world, some of the ring bruisers of the old school. John L. Sullivan still was champion and there were such old fighting machines as Kilrain, Peter Jackson, George Godfrey and Paddy Ryan. There were coming into the arena James J. Corbett, Peter Maher, Bob Fitzsimmons and Charlie Mitchell.

I was old enough to get pummeled by some Boston Irish because I favored Corbett over Sullivan, their idol. The defeat of the latter marked a new epoch in boxing. Championships began to find new lodging places, after the defeat of Sullivan who was perhaps one of the greatest of fighters. With Corbett there came a new style of ring generalship, and skill began to have a greater place in the ring than mere brute force. The world then was just beginning a stride that was to develop into one of the fastest that it had ever known, and in the fifty years of my life I have lived in the midst of that pace and still am keeping abreast of it. The chugging locomotive of my youth was considered the peak of speed possibilities, and for smart travel a fast horse was the apex of luxury. The automobile was unknown, and the aeroplane existed only in the imagination of those who were believed demented.

I have seen life moving slowly, and I have seen it as a speedy race. I do not deplore the passing of those crude old days. Present day life and the developments which have led up to it have made living decidedly more pleasant and interesting. In the fifty years of my life there has been such a rapid change in human habits and thoughts that, when the two extremes are compared, one feels that he has suddenly leaped from one form of existence to another. There has been an astounding transformation. I am not a jazz enthusiast, but I will admit that this age, which has come to be known as the jazz age is better than the preceding ages, save in a few things, and one of these to me is the great change that has come into the realm of womanhood.

In the last half century woman has attained what she is pleased to call her emancipation. She has acquired her suffrage privileges and her equal civil rights. She is rejoicing in what she believes is her independence. She has demonstrated her ability in the commercial and business world. More and more she is competing with men in every walk of life. I do not deny her these privileges. I do not maintain that she should not direct her energies into any channel that appears to offer such rewards as interest her, but nevertheless I do believe that the unrest, uneasiness and turmoil which exists in the world today, is largely due to the neglect which the home is suffering because it is being denied the thought and interest that it formerly received.

Whatever a woman's talents or rights may be, her natural place is the home. The home is the foundation of a country's welfare. From the family must emanate the men and women who must conduct the nation's affairs, whether they are of a political or industrial nature; upon the family rests the responsibility for the proper training of children and the coming generation. If home life has not been surrounded by such conditions as instill conscientiousness and respect for the better things of life, we cannot expect the development of a high class of citizenship.

Coincident with the development of the jazz age has come the flapper. She is the by-product of universal suffrage. She assumes, in the very early years of her life, equal rights with man, and insists on doing the things that men do. I am not an alarmist, but I have seen the trend of affairs. I am not seeking to destroy woman's liberties, but even if the moral foundation of the home and of the family is not threatened by the attitudes which present-day women are taking, there is one thing that is certain, namely, that she is doing things that are detracting from her feminine charm. She is coming down from the pedestal upon which man has placed her. She is losing the respect and admiration of man. She is no longer the ideal she once was, and in losing these qualities, her loss is infinitely more than she can ever expect to gain by the exercise of her equal rights.

Whether or not she and our citizenship in general are approaching a dangerous point, I will leave to any sensible, thinking person to answer. I point out that not many years ago, a woman who frequented night clubs and cafés virtually admitted that she held her virtues lightly. Today it is considered quite the thing for young boys and girls to disport themselves in such places. We wink at the situation. We accept it as a part of the new arrangement of life. High school girls have become well acquainted with the flask. They are not expected to conduct themselves any better than the boys. I do not say that boys have any more right to do these things than the girls, but I do say that when the girls make use of these rights it is not a good thing for the home nor for the future generation. I do not believe that boys and girls have as much respect for their parents today as they did twenty-five years ago, nor do I believe that the boys and girls of today are as well reared morally as they were preceding what we term the jazz age. This age I also attribute, largely, to the increased attendance of girls and women at affairs that not many years ago were patronized only by the demi-monde, and this condition I charge up to the activities of the "new woman."

In all youth there is a call for adventure. Youthful energy, untouched by the serious phases of life clamors for expression, and it will be expressed in some way. The age in which we now live limits the opportunity for that expression. The lure of night life is at hand. It presents mysteries that induce young people to cast caution aside for the thrill of exploration. It should be one of the first duties of parents to find a safe and healthful way, morally and physically to direct these energies. Young people are entitled to amusements and recreation, but they do not lie in night revelries nor in the flask. The home is the basic institution of the successful nation, and the moment the mother relinquishes or loosens her grasp on that home, that moment great dangers arise. The attempt of women to enter into public life on the scale they have, and to assert their rights by doing as men do, imperils the home.

Women should be the inspiration of men; they should be the symbol of higher attainment; they should preserve those characteristics that have always made them better than men. Woman should content herself by letting men do things *for* her, not *with* her. Once she is down on man's level, woman becomes no longer an incentive for man to better himself. He may, without dispute, grant her all her rights and privileges and aid her in maintaining them, but at the same time there creeps into his consciousness the belief that she is not much better than he, and that because she is not, there is not much use in his trying to make himself better. Woman cannot enjoy equality and chivalry at the same time.

I blame ill conditions on the new woman's activities, because with the campaign she has conducted, there have come numerous changes in life. These have reached not only into the home, but into business and social life. Along with these has come the change in our taste for music, which seems to find considerable satisfaction in the noisy and gymnastic orchestras that flourish all over the world. Theater, dance hall and night club attendance has increased many-fold in the last twenty-five years, and it seems that the jazz orchestra is the only musical form of entertainment that meets the requirements of these places. With the development of this form of music, we have lost in a great measure our appreciation of the better kind of music. Except for occasional revivals and special programs by music organizations, supported by private contributions, we would scarcely hear a composition of any of the old masters. The radio and player pianos, to say nothing of phonographs, are grinding out with ceaseless energy the latest jazz, which, while it amuses and is quite in keeping with the rapid movement of life and the lure of dance halls, nevertheless is not of lasting substance, and its inspiration is only for the moment. For my own part, I find my delight, as far as music is concerned, in the splendid compositions of the old masters, who not only wrote music in its highest forms, but who made it live with the reality of life, transferring into it such depth of feeling and such height of expression that it arouses the best qualities of human nature. One of the best tributes to the excellence of classic music, and even the old ballads and sentimental songs, is that modern jazz composers have found their themes in these compositions and by clever syncopation have, and are, giving the public the old music with its color and flavor changed.

I am neither a competent music critic nor an authority in musical composition, yet despite the time which my boxing and other interests have demanded, I have found time to learn something of music, and were it necessary I could probably fill an orchestra post. My playing, though, has been for the most part for my own entertainment or that of my more intimate friends. I mention this only because I am attempting to show in this account of my life that my interests have not been confined to boxing, bag punching and the more worldly affairs. I have enjoyed life and I have been duly appreciative of the particular talents that enable me to attain success as a boxer; but more than that, I also have looked about me considerably to see what others have attained. Whenever I have traveled in centers where artists and geniuses abound, or where their works are to be seen, I usually have found a way to visit them. Thus, I found occasion frequently, when abroad, to hear some of the great European concert organizations, which cling rather faithfully to the classic compositions, or if they gave their attention to some other form of music, one could be assured that it was of the best. Because of my interest in music and my contact with the stage, I have had the good fortune to make the acquaintance of many noted musicians. With many players and singers I have had most close and pleasant associations, and from these associations I have derived much good. Furthermore, I found that among those who have dedicated their lives to artistic attainment, there are many who are keenly interested in boxing and ring affairs, which has created on many occasions a real community of interests. Many of these artists were greater authorities on boxing than I am on music, which also impresses me with the realization that the affairs and interests of humanity are not so intensely centered as to keep us from being concerned in the other fellow's success. Among my musical friends and acquaintances I might mention the late Enrico Caruso, Tito Schipa, Titto Ruffo, and John Steele.

Aside from contact with artists, I have likewise, because of such distinction as I gained, been able to make the acquaintance of men and women in nearly all walks of life. I have been subjected to close questioning concerning prize-ring affairs by leading society women of both continents who displayed a lively interest in how it felt to be faced by an opponent bent on disabling you. I found that these women were more interested in my life and opinions than I was in theirs. More than once have distinguished women cornered me and deluged me with questions about fighters and fighting. Once in Vienna, I met the late Franz Josef, emperor of Austria, and his attendants. To be sure I was deeply eager to know something about the life of this famous old royal statesman, and if the opportunity had presented, I probably would have asked some pointed questions. The opportunity did not present itself because the emperor and members of his party out-questioned me. They asked me about events in my life which I almost had forgotten; they asked my opinion of world politics; they insisted on knowing many of my personal habits and some of their questions were embarrassing. The emperor himself wanted to know all about my life as a boxer, and listened intently to experiences I related to him.

The late King Edward of England was deeply concerned in my match with Burns, and watched the preliminary proceedings with a close eye, going so far as to utter some rather severe opinions about Burns and the manner in which he was delaying his meeting with me.

King Edward was not unlike others of the notables whom I met. He too was loaded with questions, but they were of a very different nature from most which I was called upon to answer, for he was a sportsman and followed prize-ring affairs, as well as nearly all other sport and athletic events, with the faithfulness that only a true sportsman possesses. King Alfonso of Spain, too, once surprised me with his concern in ring affairs and put me through a long questioning about numerous subjects, none of which pertained to the business of being a king, which was what I was interested in. Consequently, I learned less about that occupation than Alfonso did about boxing. Among French statesmen I numbered as acquaintances Poincaré and Joseph Caillaux. I would like to have talked of subjects different from boxing and my own life, but I had little chance —they, too, wished to know all I could tell them about the ring and kindred affairs. The late Theodore Roosevelt was an ardent boxing fan, and not only followed ring events closely, but was an adept himself in the art of boxing. The former president and I met several times. Our discussions were somewhat different from those which I have had with the most eminent personages, because between us, of course, there was a closer and more intelligent association of interests. Roosevelt displayed not only keen interest in sports but he could discuss them intelligently, and he had a fund of knowledge concerning ring events that surprised me.

I relate these incidents in which distinguished people were concerned because I was impressed with the fact on each occasion, that no matter how important they were in world affairs, nor how far removed one might imagine their interests to be from boxers and boxing, they nevertheless knew much about boxing, or at least had much curiosity about it, while I, on the other hand, knew little, but had much curiosity about them and their affairs, all of which goes to show that the human family isn't so widely different, regardless of social or political divisions.

In Europe, as well as in America, women are diverging from the old order of things. They are clamoring for independence, and the pursuit of their independence is taking them into places in which I believe woman has no place. There is one outstanding condition so noticeable that I do not believe it will be disputed when I say that the drinking of liquor and intoxication among women is increasing not only rapidly but alarmingly. Woman has become interested in politics and is a factor in many bitter disputes. In her political activities she becomes concerned with affairs that drag her out of the home, and worse than that bring her in contact with circumstances that cause her to do things that detract, as I have said before, from her charm as a woman.

At best, politics is not inspiring. It was said that the presence of women in political halls and caucuses would improve their tone and raise them to a higher level. I cannot see that it has been done. Politics continues to flourish as rottenly as before. Secret manipulations and party cunning are as rampant as before women took a hand. The only result has been to pull women down to the same level. Night clubs and political committee rooms are not improved by the presence of women—or, at least, women are not improved by being present in them, and certainly the home is not deriving any benefits when the wife and mother is raising her voice in political controversy or, in frequenting cafés.

Still another phase of the new woman movement is that which is manifested in the co-educational institutions, and even in the women's colleges. Here, young women, carving for themselves careers which they fondly believe will reach successful conclusions because of the widening opportunities for women, are indulging in parties and escapades that are shocking to the most seasoned rounder. Reports from these institutions are not based on furtive newspaper stories, but rather upon statements by faculty members and on discussions and statements by the students themselves. Petting and drinking parties, in which women participate extensively, are numerous. They defend themselves by citing their right to do these things, but granting them their right, does the exercise of this right by any stretch of the imagination suggest anything that will redound to the credit of the home? And if our young women of today do not take their home life more seriously and train to become homemakers, what will the home of the future be?

Woman's highest purpose in the world is to be loved and honored by man. It is well enough that she should have mental ability and varied talents, but these talents should be devoted to her home and to the demonstration of her superiority over man in moral perfection and high ideals. Part of her mission in life is to develop her charm and beauty, and in that she becomes the greatest glory in the world.

It happens that, as I write this chapter, the country is facing a serious situation created by the numerous suicides of college students, both boys and girls. I term it a situation because it amounts to something more than a series of coincidents. There has been an attempt to explain these suicides on a psychological basis, the contention being set up that one case of self destruction so impresses another victim, that he gives way to mental disturbances which cause him to follow in a trail already blazed. To me, the cause of this self-taking of life lies not in any psychological condition but is to be blamed upon the wholesale reaction that is taking place among young people—a reaction induced by nothing more than conditions which have been created by prohibition. Under prohibition, members of the younger generation have opportunities to indulge in secret revels in which bad liquor plays a prominent part. Do away with the necessity for clandestine drinking and vice parties, remove the conditions that make the distribution of poison liquor possible, and the moral and physical conditions of the young people will be improved.

# CHAPTER XIV

## Looking at Life at Fifty

I AM about to reach my fiftieth year. So far as I am able to determine, there never has been in the history of pugilism, or other athletic endeavors, a man whose career has been longer than mine, and there has been no one to reach my age with his skill and strength intact. Men ten to twenty years younger than I have retired from the ring and are forgotten. As for me, I am continuing daily, my physical development and the care of my body with the same conscientiousness that I observed when engaging in the arduous work of meeting all boxers. More than that, I have in recent months engaged in some severe ring battles and won all of them. Only the restrictions of boxing commissions because of my age, prevent me from becoming a contender for the highest ring honors. Yet a large percentage of the public, I believe, feel that I still am capable of standing up against the best of the boxers. Friends who know me best believe that I can defeat any of the present heavyweights.

The three members of the Illinois boxing commission, John C. Righeimer, George Walter and Paul Prehn, have told me that personally they believe I can defeat nine out of ten of the leading present-day ring men, but the commission's rules prevent them from confirming their opinions by issuing the license which is necessary, and which I believe I merit.

Denied this privilege, I am deriving much satisfaction

from persistent training of myself, and also by contributing my efforts to the training of young men who are daily working out in my gymnasium. I am teaching them to train their bodies, their muscles, their nerves and their eyes so that, whether they become professional boxers, merchants, bankers, doctors or lawyers, they will have strong bodies and good health which are assets that every man should have to make him a useful and successful citizen. If I am instrumental in helping a few of the younger men—men who must soon assume more important places in life—if I can, by my own experience and methods direct them into channels of success, I shall do more than I would in merely producing a boxing champion.

I, least of any, should speak lightly of the successes I have had and the good fortune that has been mine, notwithstanding the bitterness and tragedies that have crept into my life. I am by no means unmindful of these successes and the kindly way in which fate has treated me. Yet I believe that today I am serving in a more useful capacity than at any time in my life. My place in the world is no longer as spectacular a one, as it was a few years ago, because I have chosen to direct my path into quieter activities. These activities, I have the satisfaction of believing, are more useful to the world and my fellow-men. As for myself I am happier; I have plans and projects for the future which I think will reveal the real Jack Johnson and I am sure will redound with even greater credit to me than the things which I have done in the past.

In August, 1925, I was married for the fourth time, when Mrs. Irene Pineau became my wife. While we have been married scarcely two years this union is proving a most happy and inspiring one. Mrs. Johnson is a woman of many splendid qualities. She possesses, besides her feminine charm and grace, an unusual intellect. Her accomplishments are many and varied. Our ambitions, our likes and dislikes, our contemplation of life and its purposes, and our desires to live and live right are mutual. Between us there has developed an understanding that makes our lives peaceful, enjoyable and content, and together we are striving to attain as best we can. We have faith in and love for each other, and we look to the future with keen anticipations of the happiness and success it holds. I am intimately acquainted with the domestic life of people from all ranks of society in Chicago, in America and elsewhere, and I can truly say that there is no home filled with more sincere mutual love, peace, contentment and co-operation than my own. Mrs. Johnson represents to me the highest and the best that a woman and a wife can possibly be. At the present time I am happier than I have ever been in my whole life. My wife and I share each other's interests whole-heartedly, and these interests are not merely professional but cultural. I have every reason to believe that our love and happiness which binds our lives together is lasting. My love for my Irene is a love that knows no parallel either in my own life or that of any man I have ever known.

The more that is written and said concerning one who has held public interest, the less the public knows about that person. Of me there has been much written and much said. My enemies have never neglected an opportunity to place me in an unfavorable light before the world, which is more ready to believe the evil than the good. I do not mean this as a condemnation nor as a criticism; it is merely force of habit, a sort of instinctive desire for the sensational. Furthermore, when favorable reports concerning one's behavior or accomplishments are chronicled, they are couched in simple and unadorned terms; when a person of prominence deviates from the beaten path or even an unfounded rumor of transgression of the conventions of society arises, discussions and descriptions flare in impressive and suggestive news-stories and headlines. Sly hints of something more serious are deliberately injected and misstatements pass unchallenged. From this prevalent practice have come circumstances which have caused me many undeserved difficulties. I have been the subject of untruthful and unjust statements. I have been accused of many evils in which I had no part. When there was occasion for unfavorable report, those reports were grossly exaggerated and were accepted as true. On the other hand, when I did anything of a worthy nature or performed a distinctive service, oftentimes nothing was said of it, or, if it did receive attention, it was only of a casual and indifferent nature. I am not thin-skinned, nor do I chafe under criticism or condemnation. I have born much of it without obvious resentment. I either maintained silence or laughed it off. Yet it is not comforting or pleasant to realize that I have been misunderstood, and that my motives in many instances have been misinterpreted. I am discussing these things not in defense of myself, for I need no defense, but because I believe I am entitled to explain some incidents, the truth concerning which I know my many friends will appreciate, and which it would be good for my enemies to know.

I must admit that my profession as a boxer and my

interest in kindred matters have brought me in contact with a plane of life, the nature of which gives rise to more doubt and suspicion than attaches to ordinary pursuits. I have had associations with classes of persons who do not rank high in the social scale. For this reason it has been comparatively easy to arouse suspicion concerning me and to aggravate rumors of my alleged misconduct. Then, too, I have been the victim of prejudices and jealousies aroused because of my racial origin, and these have kept adverse criticism fanned to a heat that sometimes was intense. In all candor and without fear I ask any fair-minded and unprejudiced person or organization, if they can cite a single instance in which I have in any way been guilty of a crime or shown any inclination to criminal conduct, other than accusations arising out of conspiracies planned for the sole and selfish purpose of blocking my legitimate and rightful efforts. I challenge mention of a single instance in which I have been guilty of dishonesty, theft, bodily injury to anyone with malice, or any other crime or charge which could be sustained in a court of law.

I have been severely criticized because of my several marriages and because of my love affairs, but in none of these did I go beyond my legal privileges or conduct myself differently from prevailing customs, observed by thousands of my fellow citizens. They have involved me in scandal, it is true, and imaginative newspaper writers and maliciously minded persons have seized on them to bring condemnation and misfortune upon my head, while others doing exactly as I have, were dismissed with little more than a knowing and forgiving gesture. My marriages and my loves have been sincere. They have been clean. The women who have come into my life have been honored, and lovingly protected by me. To them I have given the utmost consideration and kindness; to none of them have I been cruel, and never was I lacking in my responsibilities for their welfare and happiness.

A pugilist is not presumed to have high ideals. By some he is believed to have brutish tendencies, and at best to be concerned only with material things. The possession of muscular strength and the courage to use it in contests with other men for physical supremacy, does not necessarily imply a lack of appreciation for the finer and better things of life. Brutish qualities and base inclinations are prevalent in all classes. A man's vocation is no measure of his inner feelings nor a guarantee of his earnest desire to live right and attain the highest standards.

Fate made me a boxer. My home surroundings when a child and growing youth were such that I might have been expected to adopt most any other means of gaining a livelihood other than boxing. As I have previously remarked, my father was a pious man and earnest in his church activities. He did not neglect to impress upon me and my brothers and sisters the importance of religious life, and I at one time was deeply concerned in the Bible and its teachings. Throughout the eventful years of my life I have never lost my faith in those teachings, but I never professed to be religious or to have church affiliations.

When I had attained distinction as a boxer and was enjoying the acclaim accorded celebrities, I found that there was much bitterness mixed with the sweetness of triumph. When prejudiced and vindictive persons and organizations began pouring their wrath upon me, and I found myself beset on every side by unjust condemnation and accusations, I sometimes wondered if there was a God. I also wondered, what, after all, was the use of attaining something if its possession was to bring persecution and cause for regret.

Everywhere I saw hypocrisy in its most deplorable forms. I saw men and women quite willing to trade their honesty and character for wealth, power or fame. I came in contact with those ready to risk their own souls and to sell mine if some worldly prestige were to be gained. Discrimination and inconsistency I found prevalent everywhere, and I began to study human nature and life in every phase that was presented to me. My attention was drawn to the churches in this study, and in following my profession as a boxer I was by no means separated from church members. In fact, they made it their business to impress me with their existence and influence, and I discovered, I am sorry to say, more hypocrites in the church and more people of church membership who were dishonest in their conduct than among all the care-free, thoughtless and irreverent spirits in the world of sport and questionable living.

In 1898, when I was twenty years old, I began to make money in quite large sums. As the years went by I made more and more money. Several small fortunes came into my possession. Altogether, I estimate that my earnings reached one and a half million dollars; yet there were many times when I was broke and found it difficult to obtain the merest necessities. It was said of me that I was a spendthrift; that I was plunging into dissipation and living a riotous life. Such stories follow in the wake of champions. My excellent health and physical condition today certainly refute these charges, because there is no more obvious fact than that dissipation and health are mutually incompatible.

But I will admit that I disposed of my money freely, sometimes wildly and foolishly; I probably spent some of it for things of no tangible value. I gave much money to churches of all denominations. I frequently was solicited by them for contributions and never, when I had money, did I fail to give regardless of creed or color. I gave my money to men and women in my world who were sick and unfortunate. I did not give in dribs nor content myself with merely giving to a special fund, but I took it on myself many times to defray the hotel-, hospital-, grocery- and rent-bills of persons whom sometimes I did not even know, but who had been reported to me as in need.

My friends and associates less fortunate than I, never lacked for anything when I had funds at my disposal, and I never thought of enjoying life, or indulging in pleasures unless those about me were as well provided for as I. I did not do these things because I wanted to be a "good fellow," I did them because I enjoyed seeing people happy and comfortable. It is with pride and satisfaction and not with boastfulness that I say that other people have enjoyed more benefits from my money than I have.

I might digress here sufficiently to mention the conventional mode of living prevalent in the prize-ring world. I seldom, if ever, traveled alone, but was generally accompanied by a number of friends and camp-followers whose expenses were paid out of my income. In this I was merely following the established custom, although I probably was sometimes not as attentive to my own financial interests and ready to cut myself loose from parasitic individuals who were taking advantage of my generosity. But looking back upon my expenditures, I do not regret the pleasures that my money has brought to those about me.

When I was accused of crime and misconduct and suspicion was being cast upon me, some of the persons to whom I had been the kindest, were the first to desert me, and others for whom I had done little proved my staunchest defenders. The churches and their members censured me severely and made people who did not know me despise me. Before I had been tried on charges, of which I was not guilty, the churches were vicious in their attitude toward me, and were responsible for much of the prejudice that arose against me. If the troubles of Job were compared with the troubles of Jack Johnson, I think that mine would be found the more intense, for they struck at my soul, while Job's greatest cause for complaint was that he had been deprived of his worldly possessions and his health, and he was moved to curse the day he was born, but I did not become so desperate as that. It was probably because I saw in the story of Job some parallel to my own experiences that he became my favorite Biblical character.

My faith was unshaken, for I believed, and still believe, that there are honest, fair-minded and decent people in the world, though I have a vague feeling that they are in the minority. Although ancient in origin and reduced to a common-place level by constant repetition, there is no greater moral or religious precept than that which urges us to "Do unto others as ye would have them do unto you," and I believe that the greatest test of our morality is to help those who are in trouble and in need, even though their own misconduct has brought their troubles and their needs upon them. I thought at one time that this was a basic ideal of Christianity, and that it was exemplified by the church and religious organizations, but I was forced to question this belief in 1913 when persecutors were hard upon my heels, and were led by the churches. The latter tried to stop me from boxing which was my profession, and they went so far as to try to stop my appearance in theaters which meant nothing more nor less than preventing me from making an honest and legitimate living. I did not mind so much that they should seek to stop the prize-fighting, for I can readily understand that churches might not believe in that form of activity. But why should they wish to stop exhibition boxing on my part in the theaters? How did they expect me to live? Should I become a thief by night, a gangster or a murderer? It was this persecution, this discrimination against me, and the insistence that I was a wicked and undesirable person which was the cause of my deeper contemplation of life, of people and the conditions that give rise to their strange behavior.

I cannot recall that I have ever been an enemy of society, nor that I have ever corrupted any one, yet here was the hand of fate in the guise of Christianity turned against me. I did not feel myself humbled, nor did I suffer a slackening of courage, but there were times when I felt that perhaps, after all, if I relinquished my career in the prize-ring I could avoid some unjust criticism. This thinking took a definite course when I was in prison. I always had given much attention to the Scriptures, and actuated by the manner in which I had been treated and concerned in solving some of the problems of existence, I gave the Bible more serious study. I became deeply interested in some of the narratives of this sacred book, because I found in them parallels applicable to present-day conditions. The result of this study was that in 1922, a year or so after I had been discharged from prison, and following the completion of a theatrical tour I addressed congregations from the pulpits of several Eastern churches.

In undertaking to address church organizations, I became the object of new attacks. They questioned my sincerity in appearing in churches. I was ridiculed and many flippant jibes were hurled at me. I was described as a prize-fighter turned preacher. To the humorists and satirists it was incongruous, and supplied their wits with sweet morsels. I was reproached with having selfish motives and accused of capitalizing the curiosity which people entertained concerning me. But if I were bent on money-making in my pulpit adventures, I could certainly have employed my time in a more lucrative manner.

In addition to questioning my sincerity erroneous reports were spread abroad concerning what I had said, and at one time I was charged with an attempt to rouse the members of a colored congregation to rebellion by advising them to use "force," if necessary, to gain their rights. In this particular instance, I had discussed casually the relations between the white and colored people, but it was from the standpoint of more harmonious living and mutual understanding, for I do not countenance racial antagonism. I would be the last one ever to appear in the role of an agitator upon this subject.

I have given much thought to the great problem of the relations of the white and black race in America. I believe that the discussion of these questions has not helped greatly to clarify the issues. White people often point to the writings of Booker T. Washington as the best example of a desirable attitude on the part of the colored population.  I have never been able to agree with the point of view of Washington, because he has to my mind not been altogether frank in the statement of the problem or courageous in the formulation in his solutions to them.  On this point Frederick Douglas'*honest and straightforward program has had more of an appeal to me, because he faced the issues without compromising.  Personally I cannot say that I have ever been in doubt as to my own policy.  Although I have often encountered prejudice on account of my race I have always, when I met people personally, been able to win their confidence by honest dealing and by straightforward and disarming face-to-face contact.  I have found no better way of avoiding racial prejudice than to act in my relations with people of other races as if prejudice did not exist.  A glance from eye to eye instantly does away with mutual suspicion.

While I was termed by some to be engaged in "preaching," I prefer to define my church engagements as lectures.  In these lectures I departed entirely from the subjects of boxing, sports and such matters as had constituted the principal concern of my life, and had for my subjects Biblical characters and narratives.  My several lectures were woven around Job, Saul, Esau, Jacob, Esther and Revelations.  I devoted several weeks to these lectures and occupied the pulpits of several New York churches as well as those of Jersey City and Pittsburgh.  My auditors were both white and colored congregations.  Wherever I went on those missions, I was received with the utmost kindness and consideration, and I have reason to believe that my efforts were not without good results.

I have taken occasion to emphasize somewhat the tend-

---

* Frederick Douglass was a slave who became one of the most widely known abolitionist editors and orators at the turn of the century.

ency of newspaper writers to utter untruths and ridicule concerning me when my conduct seemed to be not strictly in accord with moral and social precepts. I have alluded to the avidity with which the public pounced upon me when I was accused of deviating from established custom, and to the exaggerated statements, loaded with malicious hints that were made whenever it was possible to present me publicly in an unfavorable light. The press was eagerly bent upon reciting anything savoring of the sensational where I was concerned. But when I performed some worthy service there usually was complete silence. Thus, when I was in Spain during the World War, and gave my services to American and allied officials in obtaining information about the activities of German submarines along the coast of Spain, there was only slight mention of my efforts. During the war, there were a number of stranded Americans in Spanish cities, many of whom I aided financially and otherwise, and who, but for me, would have been subjected to much suffering and discomfort. But my part in these little tragedies so far as I know, has never been recorded.

I saved many lives when the tidal wave engulfed Galveston September 8, 1900. In this disaster, the greatest of modern times, thousands of persons lost their lives. As the water rose, thousands of homes were threatened and most of them were destroyed. Great numbers of persons were driven to the upper stories and the roofs to escape drowning. Avaricious men appeared on the tragic scenes with boats and wagons charging a fee of several dollars to convey these unfortunates to safety. When I encountered them, I either compelled them to go to the rescue of the victims, or brought my boxing proclivities into play and took possession of their rescue conveyances myself and piloted the threatened to safety. I spent many days in relief work after the catastrophe feeding the hungry, caring for the sick and injured and burying the dead, but industrious newspaper writers in seeking topics concerning me never chronicled these events. The records of Galveston authorities, and of the relief committees will substantiate what I have related in this connection.

A few years ago in southern Illinois a cyclone laid waste a large stretch of country. Millions of dollars' worth of damage was done and there was a large death toll. My friend, Johnnie Conners, sponsored a boxing program for the Elks lodge of Springfield, the proceeds of which were to go to the fund for the relief of the cyclone sufferers. Conners asked me to take part in the program and inquired as to my charges for the occasion. I offered my services without charge, paid all of my own expenses, and in addition paid another well known boxer a substantial sum, together with all his expenses to appear with me in the boxing exhibition. The show netted several thousands of dollars, and was one of the greatest single amounts contributed to the relief fund. Conners and the Springfield Elks lodge will confirm me concerning my part in this. To newspapers, it was only of minor interest; they would have preferred something more salacious.

At Bridgeport, Connecticut, I put on a boxing exhibition not long ago for the benefit of a sanitarium where wounded and tubercular World-War veterans are being treated. Many entertainments and other methods of raising money for the benefit of these sufferers had been tried. My boxing program made more money for the sanitarium than all the previous entertainments combined. The trustees of the sanitarium will vouch for the truth of this statement.

In an exhibition boxing contest with Sam Langford in a Boston theater I was instrumental in raising one of the largest sums of money contributed from the New England states to the sufferers in the San Francisco earthquake and fire. By donning the gloves, I was able in the unmanly and unrespected sport of boxing, according to the definition of some, to raise more money than any other single entertainment or club event conducted for the same purpose in Boston. The relief committee to whom the proceeds of this fight were turned over will substantiate the truthfulness of this statement.

Various organizations and war relief committees in England will give favorable reports of my activities during the World-War period when I was in England. I appeared in numerous boxing exhibitions, the proceeds of which were used to procure comforts for crippled, blind and tubercular soldiers. In these events I not only tendered my services without cost, but I defrayed my own expenses.

A few years ago in Chicago, while I was driving through Washington Park in an automobile, accompanied by Barney Fury, a huge car overturned pinning four people underneath. I attempted to lift the car off the victims, but injured my back so severely that I was compelled to give it up. I hurried to the Del Prado Hotel and turned in a fire alarm which brought a company of firemen to the scene. They aided me in rescuing the injured motorists. One of them, a girl, had suffered a fractured skull, and placing her in my car, I sped to Washington Park Hospital. Hospital authorities refused to admit the patient unless I agreed to defray the cost. I readily assented to this, although the girl was a stranger to me. I paid the entire hospital bill, and as far as I know, the injured girl never learned who had aided her. Records of the hospital will bear me out in this narrative.

When Sam McVey, the noted pugilist with whom I had several ring contests, died in New York City of pneumonia, I was playing a show in Cincinnati, Ohio. I learned of his death, and that a fund was being raised for the purpose of burying him. I wired to New York and stopped the raising of the fund, closed my show and followed my message to the metropolis, where I paid all of the funeral expenses and disposed of the bills that had accumulated during McVey's illness. Friends of McVey and the attending undertakers will confirm me in this statement.

During a visit in San Francisco I learned that a former well-to-do Galveston family had met with misfortune. Their only daughter had died and they were without funds with which to bury her. I went to their aid, tendering them sufficient money for the funeral and other expenses which they had been unable to meet. The mother and father, and Catholic priests who had been aiding the family, and others will speak for me in this instance.

These brief references are only a few of the many cases in which I have given my time and my money to persons and causes, in the hope of having some part in reducing suffering and misfortune. I could cite many others, but I do not wish to invite accusations of self-praise. It never has occurred to me to mention them previously, and I do so now only to present the contrast that has marked my life, and to strengthen my assertion that the world is ready and willing to make much ado over one's delinquencies, but slow and negligent in recognizing worthy qualities and deeds.

As I am writing this, almost six years have elapsed since my release from prison. These years have not been spectacular or eventful ones, but they have been modestly successful and very happy ones. When the prison gates opened, and I again found myself facing this erratic world, a new era had dawned for me. Including my prison term, I had been absent from my old haunts nine years, but I soon picked up the raveled ends. As I have intimated, I had an inclination to turn my attention to fields other than boxing, and therefore went on the lecturing platform, sold stocks and bonds for a while, devoted several weeks to theatrical work, acted as advertising representative and fostered a few small investments.

But whatever course I followed, it inevitably led back to the boxing profession in some form. In these six years, I have fought in several contests, the principal ones being outside the United States because, in this country, boxing commissions mainly animated by prejudice feel that I must retire. Besides my bout with Homer Smith*in Montreal, I engaged in some exhibition work in Cuba, and also fought two men, each of whom had gained some reputation and recognition as heavy-weight contestants. One of these was Jack Thomason whom I beat in seven rounds, and the other was Farmer Lodge, who was expected to gain more than passing distinction in the ring. I won over him in four rounds. Each of these fights, while not of great importance, received much notice, and they were attended by large crowds of both Cuban and American fight fans. Re-

* Johnson, a month prior to his forty-sixth birthday, defeated Smith in ten rounds.

turning from Cuba, I filled a few more lecture dates, one
being under the auspices of the Ku-Klux Klan organization at Danville, Illinois, where I was given a lively and
friendly welcome. At this event, hundreds were unable to
enter the hall where I appeared. My lecture topic was
"The Golden Rule," and the approval of those who
sponsored and heard the lecture was expressed in an emphatic manner. This again demonstrated to me that
personal contacts can break through official prejudices.

My outstanding ring contest of the present period
was on May 5, 1926, when I fought fifteen rounds
with Pat Lester at Nogales, Sonora, Mexico, a mile or
so south of the American border. I easily won the decision. This fight was not a spectacular one, nor did it
mean much in ring history, except that it removed Lester
from the ranks of contenders for the championship title.
He was rated as the West's most formidable fighter, and
prior to meeting me, he was considered a logical antagonist for Dempsey, who still held the heavyweight
title. But whatever this match lacked in importance to
world ring affairs, it was one of the most notable of its
kind in boxing history, because one of its combatants
was the oldest boxer ever to have entered the ring in a
legitimately staged bout for a decision. That oldest
boxer was myself. I was forty-eight years old and Lester was twenty-four. But whatever he lacked in experience, he made up in size and pounds. He was 6
feet, 3¼ inches in height, and weighed into the ring at
235 pounds, exceeding me in height by 2¼ inches, and
out-weighing me fifteen pounds. He had had three years
of intensive fighting, and had put away some of the best
men on the coast. He was being coached and managed
by Spider Kelly, a veteran fighter and manager, said to

be one of the world's greatest trainers and seconds. He had developed Lester thoroughly and carefully, and not only believed him well on the way to championship honors, but considered the fight with me only an incidental affair. The fight was promoted and directed by Dan Cole of Nogales, Arizona, and was staged in the bull-ring. More than 8,000 spectators were in attendance, special trains having been run into the Mexican town for the occasion.

Lester was a two to one favorite in the betting, because of his reputation in the west and southwest. He had shown unmistakable signs of being a formidable boxer in several hard fights. Being sponsored as he was by Kelly, of whom it was said that he seldom picked a loser, his Arizona friends wagered heavily on him. His record was good; he had a remarkable physique, strength and youth. To them he looked like a sure winner. Regardless of the odds, my friends had faith in me, and took the offerings of the Arizonans in liberal amounts. My training camp was with the 25th United States Infantry at Nogales, Arizona. All of the boxing skill of the regiment aided me in my training and officers and enlisted men backed me confidently with their money. Major Bliss, physician and surgeon of the regiment subjected me to a thorough physical examination, and watched my training carefully. He was so impressed with my condition that he wagered all the money he could raise on me to win over Lester. Because of the faith in me as manifested by these troops, and their loyalty as evidenced by their tangible backing, I had increased reason to rejoice over the outcome of the fight.

I formed a close association with Col. A. J. Dougherty, regimental commander, who extended to me many privileges and facilities for my training, and when I departed after the fight, he wrote me a letter which I greatly prize. This letter commended me for my clean sportsmanship before and during the fight. He complimented me for my "clean shooting," and declared that the facilities and courtesies of the regiment would be extended to me again if occasion presented. My training at the regimental headquarters was one of the most pleasant and successful of any similar period in my career.

Preceding the fight, sport writers had much to say about my attempt to stage a "come back." They went back into history and elaborated considerably on my unusual ring record, emphasizing my tremendous past fighting ability and unanimously crediting me with being "the world's greatest boxer and the most skillful defensive fighter ever known." The writers and boxing authorities had watched me train, and all agreed that I appeared to possess the same punch, skill and speed as when at the height of my career. They marveled at my appearance and said that I looked to be no more than thirty-two. They declared that I was the picture of health and vigor, and decided that rumors of my alleged dissipation and careless living were unfounded. "It makes no difference how strong and speedy he may appear to be, he is nearing the fiftieth mile-stone, and it is unreasonable to expect that he will be able to stand up against the strength of youth as exemplified by Lester," they wrote before the fight. How quickly they changed their tune I will show by quoting, verbatim, some of their expressions after the fight. J. F. Weadock, in a press dispatch said:

"Battling gamely, but uselessly, Pat Lester of Tucson

lost every round of fifteen in his bout with Jack Johnson, former heavyweight champion, in the bull-ring in Nogales, Sonora, yesterday. Johnson's punishing left to the body and right to the head, alternated at will, landed consistently as the men clinched. Constant clinching and infighting featured the entire bout, with Lester unable to lay an effective glove on the dusky battler. Laughing at friends at the ring-side, Johnson played through the bout, never in danger, although Lester gamely tried to land."

The report of the fight sent out by the Universal News service said:

"Jack Johnson, former world's heavyweight champion, won a 15-round decision over Pat Lester of Tucson, Ariz., in the bull-ring here this afternoon. Johnson won every round by a wide margin, hitting Lester at will uppercuts to chin and body. Lester proved himself one of the gamest of fighters by absorbing the ex-champion's punches and punishment and forcing the battle throughout. He was cut to ribbons in the third round, but kept coming. Johnson emerged uninjured and apparently fresh. The fight was fought beneath a blazing sun and before 8,000 people one mile across the American border. Spider Kelly, Lester's manager and second, failed to outwit the cagey negro, who fought as of old, apparently in wonderful physical condition and showing his teeth in a broad grin at all times. He seemingly took a delight in toying with his opponent after he found him possessed of a concrete chin and body. Lester, who has been fighting for three years, and who has never been stopped, was considered the best heavyweight in the west, but he was helpless today before the old master. As the last bell rang, Johnson requested the Universal Service correspondent to announce through Universal Service that he is back on the boards and that he challenges Dempsey or any other heavyweight in the ring."

From these accounts, it is obvious that the news writers and sport critics were compelled to eat their own words concerning the handicap of age in general and my own in particular. These accounts also indicate that Lester was no dub, and that he was not only an able fighter but a game one as well. As for myself, I came out of the ring no more fatigued than when I entered, for at no time was it necessary for me to greatly exert myself.

The fight was wholly upon merit. Both of us fought earnestly, and it proved that I not only retained all my former boxing qualities, but also that despite my age, I was a fit contender for the championship had I wished to push any claims upon that point, and had I not been prevented from doing so by the prevailing boxing regulations in the United States. I was sincere in challenging Dempsey, or any of the other heavyweights. And as I write this, I am of the same mind, but I realize that the private regulations and prejudices of boxing commissions prevent me from making a serious effort to arrange such a bout. Furthermore, I am content to remain out of any controversy that might throw the boxing business into an uproar that would do the game no good. I am willing to remain in my present place, satisfied with the successes I have achieved, but none the less eager to train and develop prospective boxers, and lend my service and experience in whatever manner I can to the welfare of the sport.

Luis Angel Firpo had challenged me to a bout in the

event I was victor over Lester, and I readily accepted the challenge agreeing to meet Firpo any time, any place that promoters might arrange. But nothing came of this prospective contest. If it had been arranged, Firpo would have presented no difficulties for me. When he was training for his fight with Dempsey in 1923, I boxed with him, gaining a full measure of his skill and ability. Newspaper accounts of our boxing were meager. The event was considered merely incidental in the preparation for the Dempsey-Firpo match, yet boxing authorities were aware of the fact that I was the master of the South American. Firpo made such a poor showing in the ring with me that Rickard, the promoter, fearing that publicity of this would injure the gate-receipts, stopped further boxing between Firpo and me.

Since my fight with Lester, a new champion has acquired the title in the person of Gene Tunney, who defeated Dempsey September 13, 1926, at Philadelphia. Dempsey, a masterful fighter, had held the championship for seven years, a few months less than marked my own claim on the belt. Jeffries also held the title seven years. I may, therefore, lay claim to the distinction of having held the belt longer than any other fighter. Tunney is the eighth man to gain the heavyweight title since John L. Sullivan, who was the first to be recognized as the champion boxer of the world, gaining that pinnacle in 1899, by defeating Jake Kilrain in the last championship battle fought with bare fists. This contest lasted seventy-five rounds, and was one of the fiercest on record. Of the eight men, I am the only one of my race in the history of professional boxing, ever to have held the title. All of the title-holders have been Americans except Fitzsimmons, who was a Cornishman, and

Burns, who was a Canadian. With the possible exception of Hart and Willard, all the champions have been of Irish extraction.

With the passing of Jeffries, Fitzsimmons and myself from the ring as champions, I think it can be said that the old school fighters disappeared. Dempsey was a link between the old battling system and the new. The former were at their height in the days of Sullivan, Peter Jackson, Godfrey, Maher, Sharkey and Ruhlin. Corbett, when he defeated Sullivan, foreshadowed the new school with his wit and speed, but the old school members had not disappeared at that time, and they made the going rough for the new fighters. Jeffries and Fitzsimmons, while they had the old school stamina, also had acquired some of the new tricks.

I define myself as a sort of composite fighter. I have contended successfully with both the new and old school products. My record will reveal that I had the strength and resistance of the former and the speed and mental equipment of the latter. And having had my innings with both, I am prepared to say that the modern fighter is not the machine that his predecessor was. The establishment of boxing commissions and the regulation of ring contests is largely responsible for this, for it permits the ascendency of men, who in the old days of fighting would never have been heard of. I concede that Dempsey was a superior fighter, but he never could have weathered the ring storms which would have swept upon him when some of the old boys, whom I have named, were at their zenith.

As for Tunney, the present champion, I believe that he, too, would have been unable to reach his present station against the onslaughts that he would have had to face, had his contestants been of the caliber of Jackson, Sharkey, Fitzsimmons and their class, if they were permitted to fight as they were in the days of their triumphs. Yet Tunney is a clever and fast boxer. He has good control of himself, and the ability to defend himself against hard driven blows. It was these qualities that won for him in the fight with Dempsey. Of these two, I believe Tunney the cleverest. I had, however, picked Dempsey to win, because everything was in his favor. He had had enough battles to keep him at ease. He had strength, skill and experience. But almost from the start he was out-boxed. Tunney, while not possessing the punch which still lies in Dempsey's glove was able to keep the latter from landing on him in a vital spot. Had a few of Dempsey's connected as he intended them, the fight would have had a different ending.

I believe I can speak as authoritatively as any one about the details of the prize-ring. It is my conviction that Tunney's defeat of Dempsey was largely due to the accidental circumstance that the canvas on which they fought was soaked by rain, which prevented Dempsey from getting a sound footing which is essential for his style of boxing. It is of course possible that Tunney might have been the victor anyway, but it does not appear to me to have been quite so probable had the boxing method of Dempsey not been so handicapped by weather conditions.

Another factor which helped to lay Dempsey low, was the form and style of his training. He was in brief over-trained. He had attempted to accomplish in a month or so what should have been attained over a period at least three times as long. He had long been out of the ring and had been engaged in occupations so vastly different from those that contribute to a boxer's form, that it was a tremendous task to get him into such condition as was necessary for the contest. His training had been intensive. Over-zealous trainers tried to restore to him all that he had lost in the months of ring idleness and neglect of training. An over-trained athlete is as sorry an object as an under-trained contestant, because he does not understand his own condition. He feels fresh and vigorous, but therein, he is tragically fooled because he lacks the co-ordination of nerve and muscle and brain, and unfortunately never realizes that something is wrong with him until he tries to achieve that which he most desires. I speak from experience. I have entered the ring in just such condition, and I am so familiar with it that I soon recognized Dempsey's handicap when his last fight started.

Charges that the Dempsey-Tunney fight was "framed" have no foundation in my opinion. Much controversy has raged on this point, and I fear that the boxing game has suffered somewhat because of these charges. To my mind the fight was absolutely square. Both men were eager to win. There was no inducement sufficient to tempt Dempsey to relinquish his own crown, because he prized it too dearly. No man would have taken the punishment which fell to Dempsey if he intended to let his opponent win. On the other hand, any financial or other consideration large enough to sway Dempsey would have so overshadowed anything that Tunney might hope to gain as to make such a deal absurd and prohibitive.

Looking over the boxers in the heavyweight division as they stand at this time, it appears to me that Tunney has the field pretty well to himself. Outside of vague speculation and idle talk, there are no immediate serious contenders for the crown. However, the boxing game is perhaps more profitable today than ever in its history. There is a great field of potential fighters and from among them it is likely that there will spring up one who will win the right to contest Tunney's title. I doubt very much that Dempsey will seek to regain his lost glory. If he does, I believe he will fail. Harry Wills continues to interest those concerned in boxing. Some persons take him seriously, but he never will get a chance at the heavyweight crown, for he does not deserve to. Although he has acquired much notoriety, he is but a mediocre fighter. There are many better than he, which was proved by Sam Langford, when the latter defeated him.

I am frequently asked if I am developing a heavyweight fighter with a view to going after the heavyweight by proxy. Perhaps I am—I do not know. It is a long way to the top, and it will take an unusual man to reach it. There are many possible contenders within my reach, and I have come in close contact with some. It is true that I am training in my gymnasium one or two men who may some day acquire the prestige necessary to challenge Tunney or some other champion. One thing is certain and that is, I am conducting a gymnasium and staging boxing bouts which offer opportunities to those with the skill and inclination. My many years in the ring and my inherent and acquired qualities seem to fit me for the direction of boxers and athletes, and in this I am finding congenial and successful employment.

As I am writing these closing lines of this chronicle I have had the unexpected and unsolicited pleasure of reading the results of a wide census of opinion as to the rank of the outstanding boxers in ring history. The result of this census is to be found in the June, 1927, number of the leading boxing Journal, called "The Ring," and shows that those competent to judge overwhelmingly nominate me as the greatest heavyweight boxer of all time. It is, indeed, gratifying as one looks back upon one's professional career, long after the events have lost their vividness, to realize that the highest authorities in the profession who have no personal interests to advance, have paid me this high tribute.

In the last half decade, my interests have been varied, but there has never been a day when I have not in some way given my attention to boxing or the training of boxers. I have had and am having many bouts myself, and I fail to see that I have lost either in vigor or speed. I do not train as intensively as I did in former years, for I have no need to do so. My principal object in doing this is for the maintenance of my health. However, my physical condition is such that within a short time I could prepare myself for a meeting with any of the heavyweights, none of whom I bar, in spite of the fact that some sport writers delight in picturing me in the act of defying the old man with the scythe. Their talk is piffle. I have demonstrated that proper living and attention to some simple rules in physical training ward off illness, or at least strengthen the system to such an extent that disease and even the weight of years cannot make serious inroads. I have proved for myself that because a man reaches the age of fifty, whether he is an athlete, a banker, merchant or lawyer, he need not give up the legitimate pleasures nor the profitable activities of life, and if in complete demonstration of this I am successful, and can aid others to attain a fuller and better number of years, I shall have accomplished more than the winning of the heavyweight championship. In fact, I feel that I am getting to be of increasing use to the world as the days go by, and surrounded by the many friends who are daily watching my progress, who are sincerely interesting themselves in my attainments, and who have confidence in me; with a great fund of understanding of the world and of people to draw on, and with the penalties paid for crimes and misconduct falsely charged to me, I anticipate the future with as much eagerness as when as a lad of twelve years, I set out to find Steve Brodie. I believe that I have much more confidence in myself than when I was demanding an opportunity to fight for the heavyweight boxing championship. My viewpoint, which was never provincial, has been considerably broadened by the varied experiences and contacts that lie behind me. My failures have made me wiser and my successes have given me great thrills and satisfaction. My half-a-century of life has been a long succession of experiences such as come to few men in our day. Between the many crises I have faced there have also been a number of short periods of calm. As I look back upon the life I have lived and compare it with the lives of my contemporaries I feel that mine has been a full life and above all a human life.

# EPILOGUE

# JACK JOHNSON

## By Mrs. Jack Johnson

IT seems fitting that I, Jack Johnson's wife, should insert some few words in this—his life story—in order to give a few facts concerning our meeting and subsequent marriage, and my impressions of him as a man and a husband.

I first met Mr. Johnson at the race track in Aurora, in the fall of 1924, and was impressed with his gentlemanly and courteous manner of speaking. He was a great deal more courtly than most men one meets. I was introduced to him by William Bernbach, a mutual friend, while I was in the company of my dear friend, Helen Mathews. Not long after this, in February of 1925, we again met Mr. Johnson. By this time I had started divorce proceedings against my former husband, Harry Pineau. Miss Mathews and I became quite friendly with Mr. Johnson through a series of meetings, and our friendship progressed rapidly, until it became an issue as to which one of us he liked best. It so happened that I was the favored one, which made me not a little happy, since my feeling for him had rapidly graduated from friendship to love. After each succeeding time spent in his company my affection for him grew, until the day came when I would have defied the world and anybody in it, to separate us.

All this time my divorce was going forward, and regardless of the many promises I had made myself to stay away from a second marriage for quite some time, because of the bitterness and unhappiness of my first venture, I now knew that nothing could have kept me from marrying Jack Johnson at the earliest possible moment, since he had asked me to become his wife.

Things went along quietly until June of that year,

when Mr. Johnson was suddenly stricken with appendicitis, and removed to the hospital. I immediately went to him, and never for one hour from the time he was operated upon, until he went home, ten days later, did I leave him. I did everything I could to make him more comfortable, and I will say that he was extraordinarily patient and docile for an ill man. I have always heard that men are usually quite irritable and complaining with even slight illnesses, but not he. Due to his wonderful physical condition, he was able to drive to Milwaukee and back just two weeks after his operation.

Shortly after this, I received my divorce decree and so —in August, 1925—we were married in Waukegan. What a wonderful day that was for both of us. I shall never forget it, nor the feeling of happiness and contentment that came over me when I was "His Wife." How different is real, soul-stirring love to that which we so often mistake for love, but which is no more than a passing infatuation. What great things are not possible, when one loves and is loved, truly and deeply.

Since our marriage, we have not changed one iota, except to have our love for each other grow stronger as time goes on. As a husband, Mr. Johnson is everything that he possibly could be. He is loving, considerate to the smallest details, generous to the nth degree, loyal and kind. To any of the people who might be a bit skeptical about marrying a man of a different race, let me say that there could not be a man of any race in the world more worthy of being loved and honored than is my husband. It took him to show me what real love and a happy home is, and in comparing mine with the lives of all my friends and acquaintances ever since I can remember, I say without fear of contradiction or exaggeration that none can boast of a more harmonious and happy home than we.

A prejudiced writer once said that Jack Johnson had a "sinister" influence over women—white women. If, to be a man, in every sense of the word—and to treat women with the utmost respect, kindness and loyalty, is "sinister," then a lot of men would make the world a better place, to emulate him, and become "sinister" too.

In a recent issue of Vanity Fair, a publication of the highest order, an article appeared by Jim Tully, in which Jack Johnson was given quite some mention. In the course of the story, the author made some statements that had absolutely no foundation. He credited Mr. Johnson with having the "affections of a 'levee negro,' " of being primitive, and of being unaffected by any tragedy in his immediate family, namely, his former wife's suicide. "Just a rollicking, happy-go-lucky negro" who wasn't worth much outside the ring, was what one gathered from the entire story. These deliberate statements of falsehoods, with no foundation of personal knowledge on which to base them, greatly aroused my anger, and I immediately wrote the author a letter, which I insert here. I could not read such malignment of my husband, and let it go unchallenged. They must know how wrong they are:

Mr. Jim Tully,
Condé Nast Publications
Greenwich, Conn.
My dear Mr. Tully:

I have just finished reading your article on "Colored Fighters," in the April issue of Vanity Fair, and feel sufficiently wrathful to write you a few lines, challenging your right to express certain things, which, I know, are merely the fruit of a highly prejudiced mind. I am referring to your statements concerning Jack Johnson, of whose personal side you know nothing, since you so obviously put down falsehoods, and convey erroneous impressions to the reading public.

Must a man, because of his color, be disparaged and ridiculed by every white man who takes pen in hand to scribble a story for the already over-prejudiced people? Cannot someone be human and decent enough to give a man his just due? You writers from whom words and stories flow so glibly, most times do not look beneath the surface to see the facts in a case.

This letter is written by one who knows Jack Johnson intimately, and who resents seeing him slandered. You spoke of his wife being a suicide, and of its not affecting her husband. Have you any idea of the hours of misery and sorrow that Jack Johnson spent over this tragedy? Must he wear his heart on his sleeve for all the world to see? Is not accepting misery stoically, a form of bravery? I think so. We call those people weak who go about crying their troubles to an unsympathetic world, do we not?

Inside of Jack Johnson's breast, beats the most tender heart, and I know whereof I speak. There never was a man who was more loyal to his friends; generous to a fault in every cause of charity, in helping those who needed help, and let me add, that many white men have been aided by these black hands. Kindliness is an outstanding virtue of this man, and loving consideration in even the most inconsequential everyday occurrences. He is quiet and gentle-spoken, contrary to your statement of his being "primitive." And in his head is more knowledge than most men can boast of. I am not alone in my opinion of him. Anyone who knows him will bear out my statements.

He has a wife who is intensely in love with him, and whom he loves equally as much; and she is proud to be married to a man who is as honestly and truly a gentleman as Jack Johnson is. She goes about with no shamed expression on her face. Instead, you will find a look of happy confidence and love in her eyes.

These things are all true. Why, then, not give credit where credit is due, and leave out all this sneering ridicule too often present in articles written for the gullible public?

How many men would willingly survive the uphill struggle, the bitterness and heartaches that Jack Johnson has had, and be the steady temperate man he is today? Few. And to what could you attribute this, but to his strong character and brave heart? These virtues have not the earmarks of a "levee negro." You are entirely mistaken in your impression of him.

Written and signed by his wife,

MRS. IRENE JOHNSON.